Bank Statement Mortgage Loans for Primary Residences

How to Buy or Refinance Your Home Using Bank Statement Income

By Joseph G. Correa

Licensed Mortgage Broker, Finibi Mortgage

Copyright & Legal Notice

Published by Live Stronger Faster

The information provided in this book is for educational and informational purposes only and does not constitute financial, legal, tax, or investment advice. Although the author is a licensed mortgage professional, the content presented is general in nature and is not intended as personalized guidance for any specific individual or financial situation.

The strategies, structuring methods, and examples discussed in this book are illustrative and educational in nature. They are intended to demonstrate concepts related to bank statement mortgage loan qualification and structuring, including deposit analysis, expense ratio application, and investor guideline interpretation. These examples do not represent guaranteed outcomes or approvals. Results may vary significantly based on individual financial profiles, documentation, credit history, property type, and lender-specific requirements.

The author and publisher make no representations or warranties regarding the accuracy, completeness, or applicability of the content and disclaim any liability for errors, omissions, or outcomes resulting from the use or misuse of the information contained in this book.

All trademarks, service marks, company names, and product names referenced in this publication are the property of their respective owners and are used strictly for identification and educational purposes only. Their inclusion does not imply endorsement or affiliation.

First Edition, 2026

Table of Contents

Introduction

Owning a home has long been considered one of the most important milestones in building wealth, stability, and long-term financial security. Yet for millions of self-employed individuals, entrepreneurs, and independent earners, the traditional path to homeownership has often felt frustrating, restrictive, and sometimes impossible. The reason is simple: conventional mortgage lending was built around predictable, salaried income—not the dynamic, often complex income streams of modern professionals. If you are someone who earns income through business ownership, commissions, contract work, or multiple income channels, you may have already experienced the disconnect between what you truly earn and what you can prove on paper. This is where bank statement mortgage loans for primary residences become not just an alternative, but a powerful solution.

In this book, you are stepping into one of the most important applications of bank statement lending: financing the home you live in. Unlike investment properties, where cash flow and return on investment often take center stage, a primary residence is deeply personal. It represents your lifestyle, your family, your comfort, and your long-term foundation. Because of this, lenders often apply slightly different guidelines, expectations, and risk considerations when evaluating these loans. Understanding these differences is critical, and mastering them can mean the difference between a denied application and a confident approval.

The purpose of this book is to give you a clear, strategic roadmap for using bank statement income to qualify for a primary residence mortgage—whether you are purchasing your first home, upgrading to a larger property, downsizing, or refinancing your current home. You will learn how lenders evaluate owner-occupied properties, how loan-to-value ratios impact your options, how reserve requirements are calculated, and how to present your financial profile in a way that aligns with underwriting expectations. More importantly, you will learn how to position yourself as a strong borrower—even if your income does not fit into traditional documentation boxes.

One of the biggest misconceptions in mortgage lending is that self-employed borrowers are inherently riskier. In reality, many entrepreneurs and business owners earn significantly more than salaried employees, but their tax returns often show lower net income due to deductions, write-offs, and strategic tax planning. This creates a challenge in conventional lending, where underwriters rely heavily on taxable income rather than actual cash flow. Bank statement loans bridge this gap by focusing on deposits and real income patterns, offering a more accurate representation of your financial strength.

However, qualifying for a primary residence using bank statements is not as simple as showing deposits. There are specific guidelines that must be met, and these guidelines vary depending on the lender, the loan program, and the overall risk profile of the borrower. For example, lenders will closely evaluate whether the property is truly owner-occupied, as this affects risk classification and loan pricing. They will also analyze your loan-to-value ratio, which determines how much of the property's value you are financing versus how much equity or down payment you are contributing. In addition, reserve requirements—essentially the amount of savings or liquid assets you must have after closing—play a key role in demonstrating financial stability.

Throughout this book, you will gain a deep understanding of these factors and how they work together. You will learn how to structure your loan application to meet owner-occupied guidelines, how to optimize your down payment to improve approval odds, and how to strategically build reserves that strengthen your profile. You will also learn how to avoid common pitfalls that can raise red flags during underwriting, such as inconsistent deposits, large unexplained transactions, or poorly documented accounts. Another important aspect of this book is helping you shift your mindset from reactive to proactive. Many borrowers approach the mortgage process hoping that everything will work out, only to encounter unexpected conditions or denials. Instead, you will learn how to think like an underwriter—anticipating concerns before they arise and preparing your documentation accordingly. This approach not only increases your chances of approval but also gives you greater control over the process, allowing you to move forward with confidence.

Primary residence bank statement loans also offer unique opportunities that go beyond simple qualification. For example, they can be used to refinance your current home, potentially lowering your monthly payment, consolidating debt, or accessing equity for other investments. They can also help you transition from renting to owning, even if your income structure has previously held you back. For many borrowers, this type of loan represents a turning point—a way to finally align their financial reality with their homeownership goals.

At the same time, it is important to understand that these loans come with trade-offs. Interest rates may be slightly higher than traditional loans, and underwriting may require additional documentation or scrutiny. But when used strategically, the benefits often far outweigh the costs. The key is knowing how to position yourself correctly, how to choose the right lender and program, and how to structure your application in a way that highlights your strengths while minimizing perceived risk.

As you move through this book, you will notice that everything is designed to be practical, actionable, and grounded in real-world scenarios. This is not just theory—it is a step-by-step guide based on how these loans are actually underwritten and approved in today's market. Whether you are a borrower looking to secure your dream home or a professional seeking to better understand this niche, the knowledge you gain here will give you a significant advantage.

You will also begin to see how this book connects to the larger framework of the Bank Statement Mortgage Loan Mastery Series. Each book builds on the previous one, and together they form a comprehensive system for understanding and leveraging bank statement lending across different scenarios. In earlier volumes, you explored the fundamentals, personal and business bank statements, and strategies for self-employed borrowers. Now, you are applying that knowledge to one of the most important use cases: your primary residence.

By the end of this book, you will not only understand how to qualify for a mortgage using bank statements, but you will also have the tools to do it strategically. You will know how to present your income, structure your assets, meet lender requirements, and navigate the process from application to closing. More importantly, you will gain the confidence that comes from understanding how the system works—and how to make it work for you.

Homeownership should not be limited to those with traditional income structures. In today's economy, where more people than ever are self-employed or earning income in nontraditional ways, lending must evolve to reflect reality. Bank statement mortgage loans are part of that evolution, and they represent a powerful opportunity for those who are prepared to use them correctly.

This book is your guide to doing exactly that.

Chapter 1

Understanding Owner-Occupied Guidelines for Bank Statement Mortgage Loans

When it comes to bank statement mortgage loans, one of the most critical distinctions a borrower must understand is the classification of the property being financed. In this chapter, we focus on owner-occupied properties—also known as primary residences—and how lenders evaluate these transactions differently from second homes or investment properties. While the concept of using bank statements to qualify remains consistent across loan types, the underwriting standards, expectations, and risk considerations shift significantly when the borrower intends to live in the property. Understanding these nuances is the foundation for successfully securing approval.

An owner-occupied property is defined as a home in which the borrower intends to reside as their primary place of living. This may include single-family homes, condominiums, townhouses, and in some cases, multi-unit properties where the borrower occupies one of the units. From a lender's perspective, primary residences are generally considered lower risk compared to investment properties because borrowers are more likely to prioritize payments on the home they live in. However, when bank statement income is used instead of traditional documentation, lenders introduce additional layers of scrutiny to ensure that the borrower's financial profile supports the loan.

One of the first elements lenders evaluate is occupancy intent. Borrowers must certify that they plan to occupy the property, and this declaration is not taken lightly. Lenders may review factors such as the borrower's current address, employment location, distance between properties, and overall lifestyle patterns to confirm that the stated occupancy is reasonable. Misrepresenting occupancy can be considered mortgage fraud, which underscores the importance of aligning your application with your true intentions. For self-employed borrowers, especially those with flexible work locations, this evaluation becomes even more nuanced, and proper documentation plays a critical role in supporting your case.

Another key factor in owner-occupied bank statement loans is stability of income. While bank statements provide a snapshot of deposits, lenders are not simply looking at totals—they are analyzing patterns. Consistency is essential. Regular deposits that reflect ongoing business activity or personal income streams create confidence in the borrower's ability to sustain mortgage payments. In contrast, erratic or unexplained fluctuations may raise questions. This is why structuring your accounts properly before applying for a loan can dramatically improve your chances of approval. Clean, well-organized financial records signal professionalism and reliability, both of which are highly valued in underwriting.

Loan-to-value ratio, commonly referred to as LTV, is another cornerstone of the approval process. LTV represents the percentage of the property's value that is being financed through the loan. For example, if you are purchasing a home for $500,000 and putting down $100,000, your loan amount would be $400,000, resulting in an 80% LTV. In bank statement loans for primary residences, LTV limits are often slightly more conservative than traditional loans, particularly for borrowers with lower credit scores or higher perceived risk. Lower LTV ratios—meaning larger down payments—can significantly strengthen your application by reducing the lender's exposure.

Closely tied to LTV is the concept of borrower equity. Equity represents your financial stake in the property, and it acts as a buffer for the lender. The more equity you have, the less risk the lender assumes. This is why borrowers who can contribute larger down payments or who are refinancing with significant existing equity often receive more favorable terms. In the context of bank statement loans, where income documentation is alternative, strong equity can offset other perceived weaknesses in the file.

Reserve requirements are another critical component of owner-occupied guidelines. Reserves refer to the amount of liquid or near-liquid assets a borrower must have available after closing. These assets serve as a safety net, demonstrating that the borrower can continue making mortgage payments even in the event of temporary income disruption. Lenders typically measure reserves in terms of months of housing payments. For example, a requirement of six months of reserves means you must have enough funds to cover six months of your total monthly mortgage payment, including principal, interest, taxes, and insurance. For bank statement loans, reserve requirements may be higher than traditional loans, particularly for larger loan amounts or higher-risk profiles.

Credit history also plays a significant role in underwriting owner-occupied bank statement loans. While these programs are designed to accommodate nontraditional income, they still rely heavily on credit as an indicator of financial responsibility. A strong credit profile can open the door to higher LTV options, lower interest rates, and more flexible guidelines. Conversely, weaker credit may result in stricter requirements, such as lower maximum LTV, higher reserves, or additional documentation. It is important to understand that credit and income work together in the underwriting process—strength in one area can sometimes compensate for weakness in another.

Documentation remains a central theme throughout the loan process, even in bank statement programs. In addition to providing 12 or 24 months of bank statements, borrowers may be required to submit a profit and loss statement, a letter from a CPA, or other supporting documents that help clarify income sources. For owner-occupied properties, lenders may also request proof of occupancy intent, such as a driver's license update, utility bills, or other documentation after closing. Being prepared to provide these items quickly can help streamline the process and avoid delays.

Another important consideration is debt-to-income ratio, or DTI. While bank statement loans often use alternative methods to calculate income, lenders still evaluate how your monthly obligations compare to your income. This includes not only the proposed mortgage payment but also other debts such as car loans, credit cards, and student loans. Maintaining a manageable DTI is essential, and borrowers should consider paying down existing debts before applying if possible. This can improve both approval odds and loan terms.

As you navigate the guidelines for owner-occupied bank statement loans, it becomes clear that success is not just about meeting minimum requirements—it is about presenting a strong, cohesive financial story. Every element of your application, from your bank statements to your credit profile to your asset reserves, contributes to the overall picture. Lenders are looking for consistency, stability, and reliability. By understanding what they are looking for and preparing accordingly, you can position yourself as a low-risk borrower, even within a nontraditional framework.

This chapter serves as the foundation for everything that follows. By mastering owner-occupied guidelines, you gain the knowledge needed to approach the mortgage process with clarity and confidence. In the chapters ahead, we will dive deeper into specific strategies for optimizing your application, structuring your finances, and navigating the underwriting process. But it all begins here—with a clear understanding of how lenders evaluate primary residence bank statement loans and what it takes to meet their expectations.

Real-Life Math Example: Qualifying for a Primary Residence Using Bank Statement Income

To fully understand how these guidelines come together in a real-world scenario, let's walk through a detailed example of a self-employed borrower seeking to purchase a primary residence using a bank statement mortgage loan. This example will illustrate how income is calculated, how LTV and reserves are determined, and how the overall loan structure is evaluated.

Imagine a borrower named Carlos, a self-employed consultant who earns income through multiple clients. Carlos does not show strong net income on his tax returns due to business deductions, but his bank statements reflect consistent deposits. Over the past 12 months, his personal bank statements show total deposits of $180,000. This averages to $15,000 per month in gross deposits. However, lenders do not use the full deposit amount as qualifying income. Instead, they apply an expense factor to account for business expenses.

Let's assume the lender applies a 50% expense ratio. This means that 50% of Carlos's deposits are considered usable income. Based on this, his qualifying monthly income would be calculated as $15,000 multiplied by 50%, resulting in $7,500 per month. This figure becomes the foundation for determining how much home Carlos can afford.

Next, we evaluate Carlos's proposed home purchase. He is looking to buy a primary residence for $600,000. He plans to put down 20%, which equals $120,000. This leaves a loan amount of $480,000, resulting in an 80% LTV. This LTV level is generally acceptable for many bank statement loan programs, especially for borrowers with solid credit profiles. Now we calculate Carlos's estimated monthly housing payment. Assuming an interest rate of 7%, a 30-year fixed mortgage on $480,000 would result in a principal and interest payment of approximately $3,200 per month. Adding property taxes and insurance, we estimate a total monthly housing expense of $3,800.

To determine Carlos's debt-to-income ratio, we compare his total monthly obligations to his qualifying income. In addition to his housing payment, Carlos has a car loan of $500 per month and credit card payments totaling $300 per month. This brings his total monthly obligations to $4,600. Dividing this by his qualifying income of $7,500 results in a DTI of approximately 61%. While this is higher than traditional loan limits, many bank statement programs allow higher DTIs, especially with compensating factors.

Now let's examine Carlos's reserves. The lender requires six months of reserves for this loan. With a monthly housing payment of $3,800, Carlos must demonstrate at least $22,800 in liquid assets after closing. Carlos has $50,000 remaining in his savings account after his down payment and closing costs, which exceeds the reserve requirement and strengthens his application.

Finally, we consider Carlos's credit profile. He has a credit score of 720, which is considered strong. This helps offset his higher DTI and supports approval at an 80% LTV. The combination of consistent bank statement deposits, sufficient reserves, and solid credit creates a well-rounded borrower profile.

Through this example, we see how each component—income calculation, LTV, DTI, reserves, and credit—works together to determine eligibility. Even though Carlos's tax returns do not reflect his true earning power, his bank statements tell a different story. By understanding how to present this information correctly, he is able to qualify for a primary residence that aligns with his lifestyle and financial goals.

This type of structured analysis is essential for anyone pursuing a bank statement mortgage loan. When you understand the numbers and how they are evaluated, you gain the ability to shape your application strategically. Instead of guessing or hoping for approval, you can approach the process with clarity, precision, and confidence.

Chapter 2

Loan-to-Value (LTV) Strategies for Primary Residence Bank Statement Loans

One of the most powerful levers you have when applying for a bank statement mortgage loan on a primary residence is your loan-to-value ratio, commonly referred to as LTV. While income, credit, and documentation all play critical roles in underwriting, LTV often determines how flexible a lender will be with the rest of your profile. In simple terms, LTV represents the percentage of the property's value that is financed through the loan. The lower your LTV, the more equity you have in the property—and the less risk the lender is taking. In the world of bank statement lending, where income is already considered nontraditional, managing your LTV strategically can dramatically improve your approval odds and loan terms.

For owner-occupied properties, LTV guidelines are typically more favorable than for investment properties, but they still vary depending on several factors. These include your credit score, the consistency of your bank statement income, the size of the loan, and the overall strength of your financial profile.

For example, a borrower with excellent credit and strong reserves may be able to qualify for higher LTV options—sometimes up to 85% or even 90% in certain programs—while a borrower with weaker credit or inconsistent deposits may be limited to 70% or 75% LTV. Understanding where you fall within this spectrum is essential for setting realistic expectations and building a successful strategy.

At its core, LTV is about risk management. When you make a larger down payment, you reduce the lender's exposure. This makes them more comfortable approving your loan, even if other aspects of your file are not perfect. For bank statement borrowers, this is particularly important because lenders cannot rely on traditional income verification. Instead, they look for compensating factors—elements of your application that offset perceived risk. A lower LTV is one of the strongest compensating factors available.

Another key advantage of a lower LTV is improved pricing. Interest rates on bank statement loans are typically higher than those on conventional loans, but they can vary significantly based on risk factors. Borrowers with lower LTV ratios often receive better interest rates because the lender views the loan as safer. Over the life of a 30-year mortgage, even a small reduction in interest rate can result in tens or hundreds of thousands of dollars in savings. This makes LTV not just an approval tool, but a long-term financial strategy.

It is also important to understand how LTV interacts with private mortgage insurance, or PMI. In traditional lending, borrowers who put down less than 20% are often required to pay PMI, which protects the lender in case of default. In many bank statement loan programs, PMI is either structured differently or built into the pricing of the loan. This means that even if PMI is not explicitly listed, the cost of higher LTV borrowing is still reflected in the interest rate or overall loan terms. As a result, increasing your down payment can reduce not only your monthly payment but also your overall borrowing cost.

For borrowers who may not have large amounts of cash available for a down payment, there are still strategies to optimize LTV. One approach is to leverage gift funds from family members, which are often allowed in bank statement programs for primary residences. Another strategy is to negotiate the purchase price of the property to align with your financial capacity. Even a modest reduction in price can improve your LTV and strengthen your application. Additionally, some borrowers choose to delay their purchase temporarily in order to build additional savings, which can pay off significantly in terms of approval and pricing.

Refinancing scenarios also present unique opportunities to manage LTV. If you already own a home and have built up equity, you may be able to refinance using a bank statement loan even if your income documentation does not meet traditional guidelines. In these cases, your existing equity becomes a powerful asset. For example, if your home has appreciated in value or if you have paid down your mortgage over time, your LTV may already be low enough to qualify for favorable terms. This can open the door to lower payments, cash-out opportunities, or debt consolidation strategies.

Another important concept related to LTV is combined loan-to-value, or CLTV. This comes into play when there are multiple loans on the property, such as a first mortgage and a home equity line of credit. Lenders will evaluate the total combined balance of all loans relative to the property's value. Managing CLTV is especially important for borrowers who are using creative financing strategies or who already have existing liens on their property. Keeping your combined LTV within acceptable limits ensures that your application remains viable.

Appraisal value also plays a critical role in determining LTV. The lender will order an appraisal to assess the market value of the property, and this value—not the purchase price—will be used to calculate LTV. If the appraisal comes in lower than expected, it can increase your LTV and potentially impact your approval. This is why it is important to work with knowledgeable real estate professionals and to understand the local market. Being prepared for appraisal outcomes and having contingency plans in place can help you navigate this aspect of the process.

As you develop your LTV strategy, it is important to think beyond the immediate transaction. Consider your long-term goals and how your equity position will evolve over time. For example, if you plan to refinance in the future or to use your home's equity for other investments, starting with a lower LTV can provide greater flexibility. On the other hand, if preserving cash is a priority, you may choose a higher LTV while ensuring that you meet all other requirements. The key is to make informed decisions that align with your overall financial plan.

Ultimately, mastering LTV strategies is about understanding how to balance risk, opportunity, and financial positioning. In the context of bank statement loans for primary residences, this balance becomes even more important. By controlling your LTV, you can influence not only your chances of approval but also the cost and structure of your loan. This chapter provides the framework for making these decisions, and as you continue through the book, you will learn how to integrate LTV with other key components of your application to create a powerful, cohesive strategy.

Real-Life Math Example: Structuring LTV for Maximum Approval and Savings

To bring these concepts to life, let's walk through a detailed example of how LTV strategy impacts a real borrower scenario. Consider a borrower named Sarah, a self-employed marketing consultant with strong bank statement income but limited taxable income on her tax returns. Sarah wants to purchase a primary residence priced at $700,000 using a bank statement loan.

Sarah has three potential down payment options: 10%, 20%, or 30%. Each option will result in a different LTV, monthly payment, and overall loan cost. Let's analyze each scenario step by step.

In the first scenario, Sarah puts down 10%, which equals $70,000. This results in a loan amount of $630,000 and an LTV of 90%. Because this is a higher LTV, the lender considers the loan riskier. As a result, Sarah receives an interest rate of 7.75%. Her monthly principal and interest payment is approximately $4,500. After adding taxes and insurance, her total monthly housing expense is around $5,200.

In the second scenario, Sarah puts down 20%, or $140,000. This reduces her loan amount to $560,000 and her LTV to 80%. With this lower LTV, the lender offers a better interest rate of 7.0%. Her monthly principal and interest payment drops to approximately $3,725, and her total housing expense is around $4,400. Compared to the first scenario, Sarah saves about $800 per month.

In the third scenario, Sarah puts down 30%, or $210,000. Her loan amount becomes $490,000, resulting in a 70% LTV. This significantly reduces the lender's risk, and Sarah qualifies for an interest rate of 6.5%. Her monthly principal and interest payment is approximately $3,100, with a total housing expense of around $3,800. Compared to the 90% LTV scenario, she saves roughly $1,400 per month.

Now let's look at the long-term impact. Over a 30-year period, the difference in interest payments between these scenarios is substantial. In the 90% LTV scenario, Sarah pays significantly more in interest due to the higher loan amount and higher rate. In the 70% LTV scenario, her lower balance and lower rate result in dramatically reduced interest costs. This illustrates how LTV affects not just monthly payments but total cost of ownership.

Next, we evaluate reserve requirements. In the 90% LTV scenario, the lender requires 12 months of reserves due to the higher risk. With a monthly housing payment of $5,200, Sarah must show $62,400 in reserves. In the 80% LTV scenario, the requirement drops to 6 months, or $26,400. In the 70% LTV scenario, the requirement may be as low as 3 months, or $11,400. This demonstrates how lower LTV can reduce not only your payment but also the amount of savings you need to qualify.

Finally, let's consider approval flexibility. In the 90% LTV scenario, the lender scrutinizes Sarah's bank statements more closely and may require additional documentation or impose stricter conditions. In the 80% and 70% scenarios, the lender is more flexible, allowing for higher DTI ratios or minor inconsistencies in income. This increased flexibility can make the approval process smoother and less stressful.

Through this example, it becomes clear that LTV is not just a number—it is a strategic tool. By adjusting her down payment, Sarah can influence her interest rate, monthly payment, reserve requirements, and overall approval experience. This level of control is invaluable, especially in bank statement lending, where every factor plays a role in the final decision.

As you apply these concepts to your own situation, remember that the goal is not simply to qualify, but to optimize. By understanding how LTV works and how it interacts with other elements of your loan, you can design a strategy that aligns with your financial goals and positions you for long-term success.

Chapter 3

Reserve Requirements and Liquidity Strategies for Primary Residence Bank Statement Loans

When qualifying for a bank statement mortgage loan on a primary residence, one of the most overlooked yet critically important components of the underwriting process is reserves. While income and credit often take center stage, reserves quietly play a powerful role in determining whether a loan is approved, how it is priced, and how flexible a lender will be with the rest of your file. In many cases, strong reserves can compensate for higher debt-to-income ratios, fluctuating income patterns, or even borderline credit profiles. Understanding how reserves work—and how to strategically position your liquidity—can significantly increase your chances of approval and improve your overall loan structure.

Reserves are defined as the amount of liquid or near-liquid assets a borrower has available after closing on the loan. These assets are intended to demonstrate that the borrower has a financial cushion and can continue making mortgage payments even if their income is temporarily disrupted. Lenders measure reserves in terms of months of housing payments, commonly referred to as PITIA, which includes principal, interest, taxes, insurance, and any applicable association dues. For example, if your total monthly housing payment is $4,000 and the lender requires six months of reserves, you must show at least $24,000 in qualifying assets after all closing costs and down payment funds have been accounted for.

In the context of bank statement loans, reserve requirements tend to be more stringent than in traditional lending. This is because the income used to qualify is based on deposits rather than verified taxable income, which introduces an additional layer of perceived risk for the lender. To offset this, lenders rely on reserves as a form of financial insurance. The stronger your reserve position, the more confident the lender becomes in your ability to sustain the loan over time.

Not all assets are treated equally when it comes to reserves. Lenders typically prefer highly liquid assets such as checking accounts, savings accounts, and money market funds. These assets are easily accessible and can be quickly converted into cash if needed. Other assets, such as retirement accounts, stocks, and bonds, may also be considered, but they are often discounted to account for market volatility and potential penalties for early withdrawal. For example, a lender may only count 60% to 70% of the value of a retirement account toward reserves. Understanding how your assets are evaluated allows you to structure your financial profile more effectively.

One of the key strategies for managing reserves is ensuring that your funds are properly seasoned. Seasoning refers to how long the funds have been in your account. Most lenders require that assets be seasoned for at least 60 days, meaning they have been in your account for two full statement cycles. This helps verify that the funds are truly yours and not recently borrowed or transferred for the purpose of qualifying. Large, recent deposits without clear documentation can raise red flags and may be excluded from reserve calculations. As a result, planning ahead and maintaining stable account balances is essential.

Another important concept is the relationship between reserves and risk layering. Risk layering occurs when multiple higher-risk factors are present in a loan file, such as high LTV, high DTI, or lower credit scores. In these cases, lenders may require additional reserves to compensate. For example, a borrower with an 85% LTV and a 680 credit score may be required to show 12 months of reserves, while a borrower with a 70% LTV and a 740 credit score may only need three to six months. By understanding how reserves interact with other risk factors, you can make strategic decisions that balance your overall profile.

Liquidity strategies go beyond simply having enough money in the bank. They involve structuring your assets in a way that maximizes their impact during underwriting. For example, consolidating funds into fewer, well-documented accounts can make your financial picture clearer and easier to evaluate. Maintaining consistent balances and avoiding unnecessary transfers can also improve the appearance of stability. Additionally, keeping a portion of your assets in highly liquid accounts ensures that they are fully counted toward reserves without discounts.

For borrowers who may not initially meet reserve requirements, there are several ways to strengthen liquidity. One approach is to delay the loan application and build up savings over time. Another is to liquidate certain assets, such as stocks or investments, to increase cash reserves. Gift funds from family members may also be used in some cases, although they must be properly documented and may not always count toward reserves. Each of these strategies requires careful planning and coordination with your lender to ensure compliance with program guidelines.

Refinancing scenarios offer unique opportunities to manage reserves as well. If you are refinancing a primary residence and have significant equity, you may be able to access cash through a cash-out refinance and use a portion of those funds to meet reserve requirements. However, it is important to note that some lenders restrict the use of cash-out proceeds for reserves, so understanding the specific guidelines of your loan program is essential. In many cases, existing liquid assets remain the most reliable source of reserves.

Another critical aspect of reserves is their psychological and financial impact. Beyond satisfying lender requirements, having a strong reserve position provides peace of mind. Homeownership comes with ongoing expenses and unexpected costs, from maintenance and repairs to fluctuations in income. Knowing that you have a financial cushion allows you to navigate these challenges with confidence. In this sense, reserves are not just a requirement—they are a cornerstone of responsible homeownership.

As you move forward in the loan process, it is important to think of reserves as part of a broader financial strategy. They should be aligned with your long-term goals, including future investments, refinancing plans, and overall wealth building. By maintaining strong liquidity, you position yourself not only for loan approval but also for continued financial growth and stability.

This chapter highlights the importance of reserves and

provides a framework for understanding how they are evaluated and how they can be optimized. In the next chapters, we will continue to build on this foundation, exploring additional strategies for strengthening your application and navigating the complexities of bank statement lending. With the right approach, reserves become more than a requirement—they become a powerful tool for achieving your homeownership goals.

Real-Life Math Example: Calculating and Structuring Reserves for Approval

Let's walk through a detailed example to illustrate how reserve requirements are calculated and how strategic liquidity management can impact loan approval. Consider a borrower named Daniel, a self-employed contractor who is applying for a bank statement mortgage loan to purchase a primary residence.

Daniel is purchasing a home for $650,000 with a 20% down payment of $130,000, resulting in a loan amount of $520,000. His interest rate is 7.25%, and his monthly principal and interest payment is approximately $3,550. When we add property taxes of $650 per month and insurance of $200 per month, his total monthly housing payment (PITIA) is $4,400.

The lender requires six months of reserves for this loan. To calculate the required reserves, we multiply Daniel's monthly housing payment by six. This results in a reserve requirement of $26,400. This means that after Daniel pays his down payment and closing costs, he must still have at least $26,400 in qualifying liquid assets. Daniel currently has the following assets: $40,000 in a checking account, $20,000 in a savings account, and $100,000 in a retirement account. The checking and savings accounts are fully liquid and can be counted at 100%, giving him $60,000 in usable reserves. The retirement account, however, is subject to a 60% discount, meaning only $60,000 of its value can be considered. This brings Daniel's total qualifying reserves to $120,000.

Since Daniel only needs $26,400 to meet the requirement, he is well above the minimum. This excess reserve position strengthens his application and may allow the lender to be more flexible with other factors, such as DTI. It also provides a strong compensating factor if there are any minor issues in his bank statement income analysis.

Now let's consider an alternative scenario where Daniel has less liquidity. Suppose he only has $15,000 in checking, $10,000 in savings, and the same $100,000 retirement account. His liquid assets total $25,000, and his discounted retirement account adds another $60,000, for a total of

$85,000 in qualifying reserves. While this still exceeds the minimum requirement, a larger portion of his reserves is tied up in retirement funds, which may be viewed as less accessible. In this case, the lender may still approve the loan but could impose additional conditions or slightly higher pricing. Next, let's examine what happens if Daniel decides to increase his down payment to reduce his loan amount. If he puts down $200,000 instead of $130,000, his loan amount drops to $450,000. His monthly housing payment decreases to approximately $3,800. With a six-month reserve requirement, he now needs only $22,800 in reserves. This lower requirement makes it easier to qualify and allows Daniel to retain more flexibility with his remaining assets.

Finally, consider a higher-risk scenario where Daniel has a higher DTI and a lower credit score. In this case, the lender may require 12 months of reserves instead of six. With a monthly payment of $4,400, Daniel would need $52,800 in reserves. If his assets are insufficient, he may need to delay his application, increase his savings, or restructure his financial profile to meet the requirement.

Through this example, it becomes clear that reserves are not just a static requirement—they are a dynamic component of the loan structure. By understanding how reserves are calculated and how different asset types are evaluated, borrowers can take proactive steps to strengthen their applications. Whether through increasing liquidity, adjusting loan terms, or improving overall financial positioning, the goal is to create a profile that meets lender expectations while supporting long-term financial stability.

Chapter 4

Structuring Your Bank Statements for Maximum Approval

One of the most important—and often underestimated—factors in securing a bank statement mortgage loan for a primary residence is how your bank statements are structured before you ever submit an application. While many borrowers assume that simply having strong deposits is enough, experienced lenders and underwriters know that the way those deposits are presented, categorized, and supported can dramatically impact the outcome of a loan. In reality, bank statement loans are not just about how much you make—they are about how clearly and consistently you can demonstrate it.

When underwriters review bank statements, they are not just adding up deposits. They are analyzing patterns, consistency, sources, and overall financial behavior. Their goal is to determine whether your income is stable, predictable, and sustainable over time. This means that even if your total deposits are high, inconsistencies such as irregular deposit timing, large unexplained deposits, or frequent transfers between accounts can create confusion and raise concerns. The cleaner and more organized your bank statements appear, the easier it is for the underwriter to confidently approve your loan.

The first key principle in structuring your bank statements is consistency. Lenders prefer to see regular, recurring deposits that reflect ongoing business or income activity. For example, if you are a consultant, consistent weekly or monthly payments from clients are ideal. If you are a business owner, steady revenue deposits into your account create a strong impression of stability. On the other hand, sporadic large deposits without clear explanation can be viewed as unreliable or non-recurring income. This is why it is essential to develop a system for depositing income in a consistent and traceable manner.

The second principle is clarity of source. Every deposit should have a logical and explainable origin. Transfers between your own accounts, loan proceeds, or one-time deposits from asset sales may not be counted as qualifying income unless properly documented. Underwriters often exclude these types of deposits when calculating income, which can significantly reduce your qualifying amount. To avoid this, it is important to separate income-generating accounts from personal or transfer-heavy accounts. Maintaining a dedicated account for income deposits can make a substantial difference in how your file is evaluated.

Another critical aspect of structuring your bank statements is minimizing commingling of funds. Commingling occurs when personal and business finances are mixed within the same account. While this is common among self-employed individuals, it can complicate the underwriting process. Lenders may apply higher expense ratios or question the reliability of income when accounts are not clearly defined. Whenever possible, maintaining separate accounts for business and personal use provides a cleaner financial picture and allows for more accurate income calculations.

Expense management also plays a significant role in how your bank statements are interpreted. In many bank statement loan programs, lenders apply a standard expense factor—often between 30% and 70%—to estimate your net income. However, some lenders may allow lower expense factors if you can provide supporting documentation, such as a profit and loss statement prepared by a CPA. By reducing your apparent expenses, you can increase your qualifying income and improve your overall loan profile. This makes it important to not only generate income but also to manage how expenses are reflected in your accounts.

Timing is another strategic element that can influence your approval. Since most bank statement loans require 12 or 24 months of statements, your financial behavior during this period directly impacts your application. If you anticipate applying for a mortgage in the near future, it is beneficial to begin structuring your accounts well in advance. This includes maintaining consistent deposit patterns, avoiding large unexplained transactions, and ensuring that your balances remain stable. A well-prepared 12-month history can often outperform a longer but inconsistent 24-month record.

Large deposits are one of the most common issues that arise during underwriting. While they may represent legitimate income, they often require additional documentation to verify their source. Without proper explanation, these deposits may be excluded from income calculations or flagged as potential liabilities. To address this, borrowers should keep detailed records of invoices, contracts, or other documentation that supports their income. Being proactive in documenting your financial activity can prevent delays and strengthen your application.

Another powerful strategy is leveraging multiple accounts effectively. Some borrowers maintain several accounts for different purposes, such as receiving payments, managing expenses, or saving reserves. While this can be beneficial, it is important to ensure that the flow of funds between accounts is clear and logical. Excessive transfers without clear purpose can create confusion and may lead to conservative income calculations. Simplifying your account structure and maintaining transparency in fund movement can help underwriters accurately assess your income. For borrowers with fluctuating income, structuring becomes even more critical. Seasonal businesses, commission-based earners, or individuals with variable income streams must demonstrate overall stability despite month-to-month variations. This can be achieved by maintaining consistent averages, avoiding extreme spikes or dips, and providing supporting documentation that explains the nature of the business. Lenders are generally willing to work with variable income, but they need to see a pattern that indicates long-term sustainability.

Technology and automation can also play a role in improving your bank statement presentation. Using accounting software, maintaining digital records, and working with financial professionals can help you organize your finances more effectively. A well-prepared financial profile not only improves your chances of approval but also reduces the time and stress involved in the loan process. In many cases, borrowers who take the time to structure their finances properly experience faster approvals and fewer conditions.

Ultimately, structuring your bank statements is about telling a clear and compelling financial story. Every deposit, every balance, and every transaction contributes to how your income is perceived. By taking control of this narrative and aligning your financial behavior with lender expectations, you can transform what might otherwise be a complex or confusing profile into a strong, approvable application. This chapter provides the framework for doing exactly that, and as you move forward, you will learn how to integrate these strategies with other aspects of the loan process to achieve optimal results.

Real-Life Math Example: How Bank Statement Structuring Impacts Qualifying Income

To understand how structuring bank statements can directly affect loan approval, let's examine a detailed example of a borrower named Maria, a self-employed graphic designer who is applying for a bank statement mortgage loan to purchase a primary residence.

Maria's gross deposits over a 12-month period total $240,000, which averages to $20,000 per month. At first glance, this appears to be a strong income profile. However, the way her bank statements are structured will determine how much of this income is actually usable for qualification.

In the first scenario, Maria has a single account where all her income, personal expenses, and transfers are combined. Her statements show frequent transfers between accounts, occasional large deposits from asset sales, and inconsistent deposit timing. When the underwriter reviews her file, they identify $40,000 in deposits that cannot be clearly sourced or are considered non-recurring. This reduces her total qualifying deposits to $200,000, or $16,667 per month.

The lender then applies a standard expense factor of 50%, resulting in a qualifying income of $8,333 per month. Based on this income, Maria may qualify for a certain loan amount, but it is significantly lower than what her true earning potential might suggest.

In the second scenario, Maria restructures her accounts before applying. She creates a dedicated business account where all client payments are deposited consistently. She separates personal expenses into a different account and minimizes unnecessary transfers. She also documents her income with invoices and maintains a clean transaction history.

With this improved structure, the underwriter is able to use the full $240,000 in deposits. Additionally, Maria provides a CPA-prepared profit and loss statement that supports a lower expense ratio of 40%. This increases her qualifying income to $12,000 per month.

Now let's compare the impact on her loan qualification. In the first scenario, with $8,333 in monthly income, Maria may qualify for a loan with a maximum housing payment of approximately $3,500, depending on DTI limits. In the second scenario, with $12,000 in monthly income, she may qualify for a housing payment of $5,000 or more. This difference can translate into a significantly higher purchase price and more favorable loan terms.

Next, consider the impact on debt-to-income ratio. If Maria has monthly debts of $1,000, her DTI in the first scenario would be approximately 54%, while in the second scenario it would drop to around 42%. This lower DTI makes her a stronger borrower and may allow for better interest rates and fewer conditions.

Finally, we examine how structuring affects overall approval. In the first scenario, the underwriter may request additional documentation, impose stricter conditions, or even decline the loan due to uncertainty. In the second scenario, the clean and consistent financial profile allows for a smoother approval process with fewer questions.

This example highlights the direct connection between how your bank statements are structured and how your income is calculated. By taking the time to organize your accounts, document your income, and present a clear financial picture, you can significantly improve your loan outcome. Structuring is not just a technical detail—it is a strategic advantage that can unlock greater borrowing power and increase your chances of success.

Chapter 5

Debt-to-Income (DTI) Optimization for Bank Statement Mortgage Loans

One of the most critical components in qualifying for a bank statement mortgage loan on a primary residence is your debt-to-income ratio, commonly referred to as DTI. While bank statement loans provide flexibility in how income is calculated, lenders still rely heavily on DTI to determine whether a borrower can reasonably afford a mortgage payment. In simple terms, DTI measures the relationship between your monthly income and your monthly debt obligations. The lower your DTI, the more financially stable you appear to a lender. The higher your DTI, the greater the perceived risk.

DTI becomes especially important in bank statement lending because the income used to calculate it is already adjusted through expense factors or alternative documentation methods. This means that even if your gross deposits are high, your qualifying income may be significantly reduced before the DTI calculation is applied. As a result, optimizing your DTI is not just about earning more—it is about structuring both your income and your debts in a way that presents the strongest possible financial profile. Lenders typically evaluate two types of DTI: front-end and back-end ratios. The front-end ratio focuses solely on your housing payment, including principal, interest, taxes, insurance, and any association dues. The back-end ratio includes all of your monthly debts, such as car loans, credit cards, student loans, and personal loans, in addition to your housing payment. In bank statement loan programs, lenders often place more emphasis on the back-end ratio, as it provides a more comprehensive view of your financial obligations.

For primary residence bank statement loans, acceptable DTI limits can vary widely depending on the lender and the strength of the borrower's profile. Some programs may allow DTIs up to 50% or even 55% with strong compensating factors, while others may cap DTI at 43% or 45%. Compensating factors can include high credit scores, low LTV ratios, strong reserves, or highly consistent income patterns. Understanding how these elements interact allows you to strategically position your application for approval.

One of the most effective ways to optimize DTI is by increasing your qualifying income. In the context of bank statement loans, this often involves improving how your income is calculated rather than actually earning more. For example, reducing the expense factor applied to your deposits—through CPA-prepared documentation or cleaner account structuring—can significantly increase your qualifying income. As your income increases, your DTI decreases, even if your debts remain the same.

Another powerful strategy is reducing your monthly debt obligations. Paying down credit card balances, refinancing high-interest loans, or eliminating smaller debts can have a direct and immediate impact on your DTI. Even modest reductions in monthly payments can improve your ratio enough to meet lender requirements. For borrowers who are close to qualifying thresholds, these adjustments can make the difference between approval and denial.

Timing also plays a crucial role in DTI optimization. Since lenders use current debt obligations at the time of application, strategic timing of debt payoff can improve your profile. For example, if you plan to pay off a car loan in the next few months, delaying your mortgage application until after the loan is paid off can significantly reduce your DTI. Similarly, avoiding new credit inquiries or large purchases before applying helps maintain a stable financial profile.

Loan structuring is another key element in managing DTI. Adjusting the loan amount, interest rate, or loan term can directly impact your monthly housing payment, which is a major component of DTI. For example, choosing a slightly lower purchase price or increasing your down payment can reduce your monthly payment and improve your ratio. In some cases, borrowers may also explore adjustable-rate mortgages or interest-only options, depending on the program, to lower initial payments and meet DTI requirements.

It is also important to understand how lenders treat different types of debt. For example, credit cards are typically calculated based on minimum payments, while installment loans such as car loans have fixed monthly payments. Student loans may be calculated using specific formulas if payments are deferred. Knowing how each type of debt is evaluated allows you to prioritize which debts to pay down for maximum impact.

Another often-overlooked aspect of DTI is the inclusion of contingent liabilities or obligations that may not appear as traditional monthly payments. These can include co-signed loans, business debts, or other financial commitments. Lenders may require documentation to determine whether these obligations should be included in your DTI. Properly managing and documenting these liabilities can prevent unexpected increases in your ratio.

For self-employed borrowers, DTI optimization also involves aligning personal and business finances. Since bank statement loans often rely on deposits, ensuring that your income is clearly reflected in your accounts is essential. At the same time, minimizing unnecessary expenses and maintaining a clean financial structure can improve both your income calculation and your overall DTI. This dual approach—enhancing income while reducing debt—creates a powerful combination for loan approval.

Ultimately, optimizing your DTI is about creating balance. It requires a strategic approach that considers income, debt, loan structure, and timing. By understanding how each of these elements contributes to your ratio, you can take proactive steps to strengthen your application. In the context of bank statement loans for primary residences, this level of control is invaluable, allowing you to navigate the process with confidence and precision.

As you continue through this book, you will see how DTI interacts with other key factors such as LTV, reserves, and credit. Together, these elements form the foundation of your loan profile. Mastering DTI optimization not only increases your chances of approval but also positions you for better loan terms and long-term financial success.

Real-Life Math Example: How DTI Optimization Changes Loan Approval Outcomes

Let's walk through a detailed example to illustrate how DTI optimization can impact a borrower's ability to qualify for a primary residence using a bank statement mortgage loan. Consider a borrower named Anthony, a self-employed real estate consultant with strong gross deposits but moderate monthly debt obligations.

Anthony's bank statements show total deposits of $180,000 over 12 months, averaging $15,000 per month. The lender applies a 50% expense factor, resulting in a qualifying income of $7,500 per month. Anthony is looking to purchase a home with a monthly housing payment of $3,800, including taxes and insurance.

In addition to his housing payment, Anthony has the following monthly debts: a car loan of $600, credit card payments totaling $400, and a personal loan with a $300 monthly payment. His total monthly debt obligations, including housing, equal $5,100.

To calculate his DTI, we divide his total monthly obligations by his qualifying income. In this case, $5,100 divided by $7,500 results in a DTI of 68%. This is significantly above most lender limits and would likely result in a denial under current conditions.

Now let's explore how DTI optimization strategies can improve Anthony's profile. First, he decides to pay off his credit card balances, eliminating the $400 monthly payment. This reduces his total monthly obligations to $4,700, bringing his DTI down to approximately 63%. While still high, this is a step in the right direction.

Next, Anthony works with a CPA to provide a profit and loss statement that supports a lower expense factor of 40%. This increases his qualifying income to $9,000 per month. With the same $4,700 in monthly obligations, his DTI drops to approximately 52%. This is now within the acceptable range for some bank statement loan programs, especially with strong compensating factors.

Anthony then decides to increase his down payment, reducing his loan amount and lowering his monthly housing payment from $3,800 to $3,300. This further reduces his total monthly obligations to $4,200. Dividing this by his $9,000 income results in a DTI of approximately 47%, which is well within many lender guidelines.

Finally, Anthony considers paying off his personal loan, eliminating the $300 monthly payment. This reduces his total obligations to $3,900 and his DTI to approximately 43%. At this level, he is now a highly qualified borrower, with a strong chance of approval and potentially better interest rates.

Through this step-by-step process, we see how DTI optimization transforms Anthony's loan profile. What initially appeared to be an unapprovable scenario becomes a strong application through strategic adjustments to income, debt, and loan structure. Each change builds on the previous one, demonstrating how small improvements can compound into significant results.

This example highlights the importance of understanding your numbers and taking a proactive approach to loan preparation. By analyzing your DTI and identifying opportunities for improvement, you can position yourself for success in the bank statement lending process. Rather than leaving approval to chance, you gain the ability to shape your financial profile and achieve your homeownership goals with confidence.

Chapter 6

Credit Score Strategies and Risk Positioning for Bank Statement Mortgage Loans

When qualifying for a bank statement mortgage loan on a primary residence, your credit score becomes one of the most powerful factors influencing not only your approval, but also your interest rate, loan structure, reserve requirements, and overall flexibility in underwriting. While bank statement loans are designed to provide alternatives to traditional income documentation, they are not "low-documentation" when it comes to risk evaluation. In fact, because income is derived from deposits rather than tax returns, lenders rely even more heavily on credit as a key indicator of financial responsibility and repayment behavior.

Your credit score represents a snapshot of how you have managed debt over time. It reflects your payment history, credit utilization, length of credit history, types of credit accounts, and recent inquiries. For lenders, this score acts as a predictive tool, helping them assess the likelihood that you will make timely mortgage payments. In the context of bank statement loans, where income verification is less standardized, a strong credit score can significantly offset perceived risk and open the door to better loan terms.

One of the first things to understand is how credit score tiers impact bank statement loan programs. Borrowers with credit scores above 740 are typically considered low risk and may qualify for higher LTV ratios, lower interest rates, and reduced reserve requirements. Those in the 700–739 range are still strong borrowers but may see slightly higher rates or modest restrictions. As scores drop into the 660–699 range, lenders begin to apply more conservative guidelines, including lower maximum LTV, higher reserves, and stricter DTI limits. Below 660, options may become more limited, and borrowers may need to rely heavily on compensating factors such as large down payments or substantial reserves.

Interest rate pricing is directly tied to credit score. Even a difference of 20 to 40 points can result in a noticeable change in rate. Over the life of a mortgage, this difference can translate into tens of thousands of dollars in additional interest. This is why improving your credit score before applying for a loan can be one of the most effective financial moves you can make. Unlike income, which may take time to increase, credit score improvements can often be achieved relatively quickly through targeted strategies. One of the most impactful ways to improve your credit score is by managing credit utilization. Utilization refers to the percentage of your available credit that you are currently using. For example, if you have a credit card with a $10,000 limit and a $5,000 balance, your utilization is 50%. Lenders prefer to see utilization below 30%, and ideally below 10% for optimal scoring. Paying down credit card balances can result in rapid score improvements, often within one reporting cycle. This makes it a powerful tool for borrowers preparing to apply for a mortgage.

Payment history is another critical factor. Late payments, collections, and charge-offs can significantly impact your score and raise concerns for lenders. While past issues cannot always be removed, demonstrating a consistent pattern of on-time payments in recent months can help rebuild credibility. For borrowers with prior credit challenges, time and consistency are key. Lenders often look at the recency of negative events, with older issues carrying less weight than recent ones.

Credit inquiries and new accounts also play a role in your score. Opening new lines of credit or applying for multiple loans in a short period can temporarily lower your score and signal increased risk. For this reason, it is generally advisable to avoid new credit activity in the months leading up to a mortgage application. Maintaining stability in your credit profile helps present a consistent and reliable financial picture. Another important consideration is the mix of credit accounts. A diverse credit profile that includes both revolving accounts (such as credit cards) and installment loans (such as auto loans or mortgages) can positively influence your score. However, this factor is less significant than utilization and payment history. The key is to manage existing accounts responsibly rather than opening new ones solely to improve your mix.

For self-employed borrowers, credit also serves as a balancing factor against nontraditional income. If your bank statements show strong deposits but your credit score is lower, lenders may view the overall profile as higher risk. Conversely, a high credit score can offset minor inconsistencies in income or documentation. This interplay between credit and income highlights the importance of viewing your application holistically rather than focusing on a single element.

Risk positioning goes beyond just your score—it involves how your entire credit profile is presented. For example, having multiple accounts with small balances may be viewed more favorably than having one account with a high balance. Similarly, a long history of stable credit usage demonstrates reliability. By understanding how lenders interpret these patterns, you can make strategic adjustments that enhance your overall profile. Rapid rescore is another tool that can be used in certain situations. This process allows lenders to update your credit report quickly after changes have been made, such as paying down balances or correcting errors. While not always necessary, rapid rescore can be valuable for borrowers who are close to qualifying thresholds and need a quick boost in their score.

It is also important to address any errors or inaccuracies on your credit report. Mistakes such as incorrect balances, duplicate accounts, or outdated negative items can negatively impact your score. Reviewing your credit report in advance and disputing any errors ensures that your score accurately reflects your financial behavior.

Ultimately, credit score strategies are about control and preparation. By understanding how your score is calculated and how it influences your loan, you can take proactive steps to improve your position. In the context of bank statement loans for primary residences, this preparation can lead to better approval outcomes, lower costs, and a smoother overall process.

As you continue through this book, you will see how credit interacts with other factors such as DTI, LTV, and reserves. Together, these elements form a comprehensive risk profile that lenders use to make decisions. Mastering credit strategies allows you to strengthen this profile and move forward with confidence in your homeownership journey.

Real-Life Math Example: How Credit Score Impacts Loan Cost and Approval

To illustrate the impact of credit score on a bank statement mortgage loan, let's examine a detailed example involving a borrower named David, a self-employed business owner purchasing a primary residence.

David is buying a home for $600,000 with a 20% down payment of $120,000, resulting in a loan amount of $480,000. His monthly housing payment, including taxes and insurance, is estimated at $3,800. His bank statement income qualifies him comfortably for this payment, so the primary variable in this example is his credit score.

In the first scenario, David has a credit score of 760. With this strong score, he qualifies for an interest rate of 6.75%. His monthly principal and interest payment is approximately $3,115, and his total housing payment remains around $3,800. Over a 30-year term, his total interest paid is approximately $640,000.

In the second scenario, David's credit score is 700. With this lower score, his interest rate increases to 7.25%. His monthly principal and interest payment rises to approximately $3,275, increasing his total housing payment to around $3,960. Over 30 years, his total interest paid increases to approximately $700,000. This represents an additional $60,000 in interest compared to the first scenario.

In the third scenario, David's credit score drops to 660. His interest rate increases further to 7.75%, resulting in a monthly principal and interest payment of approximately $3,450 and a total housing payment of around $4,150. Over the life of the loan, his total interest paid exceeds $760,000, adding more than $120,000 in additional cost compared to the 760 score scenario.

Now let's examine how credit score impacts approval flexibility. In the 760 score scenario, David may qualify for higher DTI limits, lower reserve requirements, and faster underwriting approval. In the 700 score scenario, the lender may require slightly higher reserves or impose additional conditions. In the 660 score scenario, the lender may reduce the maximum allowable LTV, require more reserves, or even limit the loan options available.

Next, consider how a simple credit improvement strategy can change the outcome. Suppose David pays down his credit card balances, reducing his utilization from 60% to 20%. This increases his score from 660 to 720 within a short period. As a result, his interest rate improves to approximately 7.0%, reducing his monthly payment and total interest cost significantly.

Finally, let's look at the combined impact of credit and DTI. With a higher credit score, lenders may allow David to qualify with a higher DTI, giving him more flexibility in choosing a home or managing other debts. This demonstrates how credit not only affects cost but also expands your options.

Through this example, it becomes clear that credit score is more than just a number—it is a critical driver of both affordability and approval. By taking proactive steps to improve and manage your credit, you can significantly enhance your loan outcome and achieve your homeownership goals more efficiently.

Chapter 7

Interest Rates, Pricing Adjustments, and Loan Structure Optimization

When it comes to bank statement mortgage loans for primary residences, one of the most misunderstood—and most important—components of the entire process is how interest rates are determined and how loan pricing is structured. Many borrowers focus primarily on approval, assuming that once they qualify, the rest of the process is straightforward. However, the reality is that interest rates, pricing adjustments, and loan structure decisions can have a profound impact on your monthly payment, total cost of the loan, and long-term financial outcomes. Understanding how these elements work allows you to move beyond simply qualifying and begin optimizing your mortgage for both affordability and wealth-building.

Interest rates in bank statement loan programs are not fixed in the same way as traditional agency loans. Instead, they are highly sensitive to risk factors. Lenders evaluate your entire financial profile—credit score, loan-to-value ratio, debt-to-income ratio, reserves, property type, and income consistency—to determine your pricing tier. Each of these factors contributes to what is known as risk-based pricing. The stronger your overall profile, the lower your interest rate is likely to be. Conversely, higher perceived risk results in higher rates.

One of the primary drivers of interest rate is credit score. As discussed in the previous chapter, higher credit scores signal lower risk and lead to more favorable pricing. However, credit is only one piece of the puzzle. Loan-to-value ratio also plays a major role. Borrowers with lower LTV ratios—meaning they are putting more money down—typically receive better rates because the lender's exposure is reduced. This is why increasing your down payment can be a powerful strategy not only for approval but also for cost reduction.

Debt-to-income ratio also influences pricing, although sometimes indirectly. While DTI is primarily used for qualification, higher DTIs can push a borrower into a higher risk category, which may result in rate adjustments. Similarly, reserve levels can affect pricing. Borrowers with strong reserves demonstrate financial stability, which can lead to more favorable terms. In this way, all elements of your loan profile are interconnected, and improvements in one area can positively impact others.

Another important concept is rate versus points. In many bank statement loan programs, borrowers have the option to adjust their interest rate by paying discount points upfront. A point is typically equal to 1% of the loan amount. Paying points can lower your interest rate, which reduces your monthly payment and total interest over time. However, it requires additional cash at closing. Deciding whether to pay points involves analyzing how long you plan to keep the loan and calculating the break-even point—the time it takes for the monthly savings to offset the upfront cost.

Loan term is another critical factor in structuring your mortgage. While 30-year fixed loans are the most common, some borrowers may consider 15-year terms or adjustable-rate mortgages (ARMs). A shorter loan term generally comes with a lower interest rate and faster equity buildup but higher monthly payments. An ARM may offer a lower initial rate, which can improve affordability in the short term, but it introduces the risk of future rate adjustments. Choosing the right loan term requires balancing your current financial situation with your long-term goals.

Interest-only options are sometimes available in bank statement loan programs, particularly for higher-income borrowers or those seeking to maximize cash flow. With an interest-only loan, the borrower pays only the interest for a specified period, resulting in a lower initial monthly payment. This can be beneficial for borrowers who expect their income to increase or who plan to refinance or sell the property within a few years. However, it is important to understand that the principal balance does not decrease during the interest-only period, which affects long-term equity.

Another key element of pricing is lender overlays. These are additional guidelines or adjustments that individual lenders apply on top of standard program requirements. Overlays can affect everything from minimum credit scores to maximum LTV and pricing adjustments. This is why working with a knowledgeable mortgage professional who understands different lender options can be invaluable. The same borrower profile may receive significantly different terms from different lenders.

Market conditions also play a role in interest rate determination. Factors such as inflation, economic growth, and central bank policies influence overall mortgage rates. While these factors are beyond your control, understanding their impact can help you make informed decisions about timing. In some cases, locking in a rate at the right time can result in substantial savings.

Locking your interest rate is another strategic decision. A rate lock guarantees your interest rate for a specified period, typically 30 to 60 days, while your loan is processed. This protects you from market fluctuations but may come with a cost if extended. Deciding when to lock your rate involves balancing the risk of rising rates against the possibility of lower rates in the future.

Fee structures also contribute to the overall cost of your loan. In addition to interest, borrowers must consider origination fees, underwriting fees, appraisal costs, and other closing expenses. Some lenders offer "no-cost" options where fees are rolled into the interest rate. While this can reduce upfront costs, it typically results in a higher rate. Evaluating the trade-off between upfront costs and long-term expenses is essential for making the best decision.

Ultimately, optimizing your loan structure is about aligning your mortgage with your financial strategy. Whether your goal is to minimize monthly payments, reduce total interest, maximize cash flow, or build equity quickly, the choices you make in structuring your loan will determine your outcome. By understanding how interest rates and pricing adjustments work, you gain the ability to make informed decisions that support your long-term goals.

This chapter emphasizes that your mortgage is not just a loan—it is a financial tool. When used strategically, it can enhance your financial position and create opportunities for growth. As you continue through this book, you will learn how to integrate these concepts with other aspects of bank statement lending to build a comprehensive and effective approach to homeownership.

Real-Life Math Example: Comparing Loan Structures and Pricing Strategies

To illustrate how interest rates and loan structure decisions impact a borrower's financial outcome, let's examine a detailed example involving a borrower named Lisa, a self-employed entrepreneur purchasing a primary residence.

Lisa is buying a home for $650,000 with a 20% down payment of $130,000, resulting in a loan amount of $520,000. She has a strong credit profile and qualifies for multiple loan options. Let's compare three different scenarios: a standard 30-year fixed loan, a discounted rate with points, and an adjustable-rate mortgage.

In the first scenario, Lisa chooses a 30-year fixed loan with an interest rate of 7.25%. Her monthly principal and interest payment is approximately $3,550. Over 30 years, she will pay approximately $758,000 in total interest.

In the second scenario, Lisa decides to pay one discount point, which costs 1% of the loan amount, or $5,200. In exchange, her interest rate is reduced to 6.75%. Her monthly payment drops to approximately $3,375, saving her $175 per month. Over time, this reduction results in significant interest savings. To calculate the break-even point, we divide the upfront cost by the monthly savings. In this case, $5,200 divided by $175 equals approximately 30 months. This means that if Lisa keeps the loan for more than 2.5 years, she benefits from paying the point.

In the third scenario, Lisa chooses a 5/6 adjustable-rate mortgage with an initial rate of 6.25%. Her monthly payment is approximately $3,200, saving her $350 per month compared to the fixed-rate option. However, after five years, the rate may adjust based on market conditions. If rates increase, her payment could rise significantly. This option provides short-term savings but introduces long-term uncertainty.

Now let's consider the impact of LTV adjustments. If Lisa increases her down payment to 30%, reducing her loan amount to $455,000, her interest rate may drop to 6.75% even without paying points. Her monthly payment would decrease further, and her total interest cost would be significantly lower. This demonstrates how combining strategies—such as increasing down payment and optimizing rate—can amplify benefits.

Next, we evaluate total cost over time. In the fixed-rate scenario at 7.25%, Lisa pays the highest total interest. In the discounted rate scenario, she pays less interest after the break-even point. In the ARM scenario, she saves the most in the short term but faces potential increases later. Each option has trade-offs, and the best choice depends on Lisa's financial goals and how long she plans to keep the loan.

Finally, we consider cash flow versus long-term savings. If Lisa prioritizes lower monthly payments, the ARM or discounted rate options may be more attractive. If she prioritizes stability and predictability, the fixed-rate loan may be the better choice. By analyzing these scenarios, Lisa can make an informed decision that aligns with her overall financial strategy.

This example highlights the importance of understanding how loan structure and pricing decisions affect both immediate affordability and long-term cost. By evaluating multiple scenarios and calculating the impact of each option, borrowers can move beyond basic qualification and create a mortgage strategy that supports their financial success.

Chapter 8

The Underwriting Process and How to Navigate Conditions Successfully

Once you have structured your income, optimized your credit, aligned your debt-to-income ratio, and positioned your loan-to-value and reserves correctly, you enter one of the most critical stages of the mortgage process: underwriting. For many borrowers, underwriting feels like a black box—documents go in, questions come out, and decisions are made behind the scenes. However, for those who understand how underwriting works, this stage becomes far less intimidating and far more strategic. In bank statement mortgage loans for primary residences, underwriting is where your entire financial story is evaluated, verified, and ultimately approved or declined.

Underwriting is the process by which a lender assesses the risk of a loan by reviewing all aspects of the borrower's financial profile. This includes income, assets, credit, property details, and overall loan structure. In traditional loans, underwriters rely heavily on tax returns and standardized income calculations. In bank statement loans, however, underwriters take a more analytical approach, focusing on deposit trends, consistency, and the overall credibility of the borrower's financial narrative. This makes preparation and presentation even more important.

The underwriting process typically begins after your loan application has been submitted and your initial documents have been reviewed by a loan processor. At this stage, the file is handed off to an underwriter, who conducts a detailed evaluation. The underwriter's job is not to approve or deny arbitrarily—it is to ensure that the loan meets all program guidelines and that the borrower has the ability and willingness to repay the loan. Every document you provide is analyzed with this objective in mind.

One of the most important concepts to understand is that underwriting is condition-based. Rarely is a loan approved without conditions. Instead, the underwriter issues a conditional approval, which outlines specific items that must be addressed before final approval can be granted. These conditions can range from simple document requests to more complex clarifications. Successfully navigating these conditions is the key to moving your loan from approval to closing.

Common underwriting conditions in bank statement loans include requests for additional bank statements, explanations for large deposits, verification of business activity, and clarification of income sources. For example, if an underwriter identifies a large deposit that does not match your typical income pattern, they may request documentation such as invoices, contracts, or a letter of explanation. Being prepared to provide these documents quickly and clearly can significantly speed up the process.

Another frequent condition involves consistency of income. Underwriters may analyze your bank statements to ensure that deposits are stable over time. If there are fluctuations, they may ask for explanations or additional documentation to confirm that the income is ongoing. This is particularly common for borrowers with seasonal or variable income. Providing context—such as the nature of your business or industry trends—can help the underwriter understand and accept these variations.

Asset verification is another critical component of underwriting. Lenders must confirm that you have sufficient funds for your down payment, closing costs, and reserves. This includes verifying the source of funds and ensuring that they are seasoned. Large or recent deposits may require documentation to confirm that they are not borrowed funds. Maintaining clear and well-documented accounts simplifies this process and reduces the likelihood of delays.

Occupancy verification is especially important for primary residence loans. Underwriters may review your application to ensure that the property will indeed be your primary home. This can involve reviewing your current address, employment location, and overall living situation. In some cases, additional documentation may be required to support your intent to occupy the property. Ensuring that your application aligns with your actual plans is essential for avoiding complications.

Communication plays a vital role in navigating underwriting conditions. Responding promptly to requests, providing clear and complete documentation, and maintaining open communication with your loan officer can make a significant difference in the speed and success of your loan. Delays often occur when conditions are not fully addressed or when documentation is incomplete. Taking a proactive approach helps keep the process moving forward.

Another important aspect of underwriting is the concept of "story." Underwriters are not just reviewing numbers—they are evaluating the overall narrative of your financial situation. A well-organized file with consistent information tells a clear story and builds confidence. In contrast, a file with discrepancies, missing information, or unclear transactions creates uncertainty. Your goal is to present a cohesive and logical financial picture that aligns with lender expectations.

Appraisal is also part of the underwriting process. The lender orders an appraisal to determine the value of the property and ensure that it supports the loan amount. If the appraisal comes in lower than expected, it can impact your LTV and require adjustments to your loan structure. Being prepared for this possibility and having contingency plans in place can help you navigate this step successfully.

Final approval, often referred to as "clear to close," occurs once all conditions have been satisfied and the underwriter is confident that the loan meets all requirements. At this stage, the file moves to closing, where final documents are prepared and signed. Reaching this point requires careful attention to detail and a disciplined approach to addressing conditions.

Ultimately, underwriting is not something to fear—it is something to understand and manage. By knowing what underwriters are looking for and preparing accordingly, you can turn this stage into an opportunity to demonstrate your strength as a borrower. In bank statement lending, where the process is more nuanced, this understanding becomes even more valuable.

This chapter provides you with the tools and insights needed to navigate underwriting with confidence. As you apply these principles, you will find that the process becomes more predictable, more efficient, and ultimately more successful. With the right preparation and mindset, you can move through underwriting smoothly and reach your goal of homeownership.

Real-Life Math Example: How Underwriting Conditions Impact Loan Approval

To illustrate how underwriting works in practice, let's examine a detailed example involving a borrower named Kevin, a self-employed consultant applying for a bank statement mortgage loan to purchase a primary residence.

Kevin is purchasing a home for $550,000 with a 20% down payment of $110,000, resulting in a loan amount of $440,000. His bank statements show total deposits of $144,000 over 12 months, averaging $12,000 per month. The lender applies a 50% expense factor, resulting in a qualifying income of $6,000 per month.

Kevin's estimated monthly housing payment, including taxes and insurance, is $3,200. He also has a car payment of $500 and credit card payments totaling $300. His total monthly obligations are $4,000. Dividing this by his qualifying income of $6,000 results in a DTI of approximately 67%, which is higher than most program limits.

During underwriting, the underwriter identifies several conditions. First, they note that $20,000 of Kevin's deposits come from large, irregular transactions. These deposits cannot be clearly sourced and are excluded from income calculations. This reduces his total qualifying deposits to $124,000, or approximately $10,333 per month. Applying the 50% expense factor results in a new qualifying income of $5,166 per month.

With this adjusted income, Kevin's DTI increases to approximately 77%, making the loan ineligible under current conditions. To address this, Kevin must take corrective action. He provides documentation for the large deposits, including invoices and contracts, which allows the underwriter to include them in the income calculation. This restores his qualifying income to $6,000 per month.

Next, Kevin decides to pay off his credit card balances, eliminating the $300 monthly payment. This reduces his total monthly obligations to $3,700. Dividing this by his $6,000 income results in a DTI of approximately 62%. While still high, this is closer to acceptable limits.

To further improve his profile, Kevin increases his down payment to $140,000, reducing his loan amount to $410,000. This lowers his monthly housing payment to approximately

$3,000. His total monthly obligations now drop to $3,500, resulting in a DTI of approximately 58%.

Finally, Kevin provides additional reserves, demonstrating 12 months of housing payments in liquid assets. This strong reserve position acts as a compensating factor, allowing the lender to approve the loan despite the higher DTI.

Through this example, we see how underwriting conditions directly impact loan approval and how strategic adjustments can resolve issues. Each step—documenting deposits, reducing debt, adjusting loan structure, and strengthening reserves—contributes to a successful outcome.

This process highlights the importance of understanding underwriting as a dynamic and interactive stage. Rather than being a passive process, it requires active participation and strategic decision-making. By approaching underwriting with preparation and flexibility, borrowers can overcome challenges and achieve approval, even in complex scenarios.

Chapter 9

Overcoming Credit Challenges and Structuring Compensating Factors

In the world of bank statement mortgage loans for primary residences, not every borrower begins the process with a perfect financial profile. In fact, many of the individuals who benefit most from these programs are those who have experienced credit challenges at some point in their financial journey. Whether it is a past late payment, a collection account, a prior bankruptcy, or a foreclosure, these events can create obstacles in traditional lending. However, bank statement loan programs are designed with flexibility in mind, allowing borrowers to qualify based on their current financial strength rather than being permanently defined by past setbacks. The key lies in understanding how to position your application using compensating factors.

Compensating factors are strengths in your financial profile that offset areas of perceived risk. In the context of credit challenges, they become essential tools for achieving approval. Lenders are not simply looking for perfection—they are looking for balance. If one area of your application presents risk, other areas must demonstrate strength to create a well-rounded and acceptable profile. This chapter focuses on how to identify, build, and leverage these compensating factors to overcome credit-related obstacles.

One of the most important aspects of addressing credit challenges is understanding the concept of seasoning. Seasoning refers to the amount of time that has passed since a negative credit event occurred. Lenders typically require specific waiting periods for events such as bankruptcies, foreclosures, or short sales. For example, a borrower may need to wait two to four years after a major credit event before qualifying for certain programs. However, within bank statement lending, these timelines can sometimes be more flexible, especially if the borrower has demonstrated strong financial behavior since the event. The longer the seasoning period, the less impact the event has on underwriting.

Equally important is the borrower's recent credit history. Lenders place significant emphasis on what you have done lately. A borrower who had credit issues several years ago but has maintained a perfect payment history over the past 12 to 24 months presents a much stronger profile than someone with recent delinquencies. Consistency and reliability in recent credit behavior signal that past issues have been resolved and are unlikely to recur. Credit score itself remains a central factor, but it should be viewed in context. A lower credit score does not automatically result in denial. Instead, it shifts the focus to other areas of the application. For example, a borrower with a 660 credit score may still qualify if they have a low LTV, strong reserves, and stable income. In this way, the credit score becomes one piece of a larger puzzle rather than the sole determining factor.

Loan-to-value ratio is one of the most powerful compensating factors for credit challenges. By increasing your down payment or leveraging existing equity, you reduce the lender's risk. A lower LTV demonstrates commitment and financial stability, making lenders more comfortable approving the loan. For borrowers with credit issues, targeting a lower LTV can significantly improve approval odds and potentially offset higher interest rates.

Reserves also play a critical role in compensating for credit challenges. Demonstrating that you have substantial liquid assets after closing provides reassurance that you can handle unexpected expenses or temporary income disruptions. In many cases, lenders may require additional reserves for borrowers with lower credit scores. By exceeding these requirements, you strengthen your application and create a buffer against perceived risk.

Income stability is another key factor. For bank statement loans, this means showing consistent and reliable deposits over time. Even if your credit history has imperfections, strong income patterns can demonstrate your ability to repay the loan. Lenders are particularly interested in trends—steady or increasing income over a 12- or 24-month period is viewed favorably. Structuring your bank statements to highlight this consistency is essential.

Documentation and transparency are especially important when addressing credit challenges. Lenders may request letters of explanation for past credit events, detailing the circumstances and how they have been resolved. These letters should be clear, concise, and honest. Providing supporting documentation, such as proof of hardship or evidence of financial recovery, can further strengthen your case. The goal is to show that the issue was temporary and that your current financial situation is stable.

Another strategy involves reducing overall risk by simplifying your financial profile. This can include paying down existing debts, avoiding new credit inquiries, and maintaining stable account balances. The fewer variables in your application, the easier it is for the underwriter to evaluate and approve your loan. Simplicity and clarity are powerful tools in overcoming credit challenges. For borrowers with more significant credit issues, such as recent bankruptcies or foreclosures, working with specialized lenders may be necessary. These lenders are experienced in evaluating complex profiles and may offer programs tailored to borrowers with unique circumstances. While terms may be less favorable initially, these loans can serve as a stepping stone, allowing borrowers to rebuild their credit and refinance into better terms in the future.

It is also important to adopt a long-term perspective. Overcoming credit challenges is not just about securing a loan—it is about rebuilding financial strength and creating a foundation for future opportunities. By improving your credit, managing your finances responsibly, and leveraging compensating factors, you position yourself for continued success beyond the initial transaction.

Ultimately, this chapter emphasizes that credit challenges are not insurmountable barriers. With the right strategies, preparation, and mindset, they can be managed and overcome. Bank statement mortgage loans provide a pathway for borrowers who may not fit traditional criteria, and by understanding how to use compensating factors effectively, you can navigate this path with confidence and achieve your homeownership goals.

Real-Life Math Example: Using Compensating Factors to Overcome Credit Challenges

To illustrate how compensating factors can transform a challenging credit profile into an approvable loan, let's examine a detailed example involving a borrower named Jessica, a self-employed business owner seeking to purchase a primary residence.

Jessica is purchasing a home for $500,000. She initially plans to put down 10%, or $50,000, resulting in a loan amount of $450,000 and an LTV of 90%. Her bank statements show total deposits of $120,000 over 12 months, averaging $10,000 per month. The lender applies a 50% expense factor, resulting in a qualifying income of $5,000 per month.

Jessica's estimated monthly housing payment is $3,200. She also has a car loan of $400 and credit card payments totaling $300, bringing her total monthly obligations to $3,900. Dividing this by her income of $5,000 results in a DTI of 78%, which is too high for most programs. Additionally, Jessica has a credit score of 660 due to a bankruptcy that occurred three years ago.

In this initial scenario, Jessica's loan is unlikely to be approved. However, by applying compensating factor strategies, she can significantly improve her profile. First,

Jessica increases her down payment to 25%, or $125,000. This reduces her loan amount to $375,000 and her LTV to 75%. Her monthly housing payment drops to approximately $2,700. This lower LTV reduces the lender's risk and improves her overall profile.

Next, Jessica pays off her credit card balances, eliminating the $300 monthly payment. Her total monthly obligations are now $3,100. Dividing this by her $5,000 income results in a DTI of 62%, which is still high but closer to acceptable limits.

Jessica then works with a CPA to provide a profit and loss statement that supports a lower expense factor of 40%. This increases her qualifying income to $6,000 per month. With $3,100 in monthly obligations, her DTI drops to approximately 52%, which falls within the acceptable range for some bank statement programs.

To further strengthen her application, Jessica demonstrates 12 months of reserves, totaling approximately $32,400 based on her housing payment. This strong reserve position acts as a significant compensating factor, providing additional assurance to the lender.

Finally, Jessica provides a letter of explanation for her bankruptcy, along with documentation showing that it was caused by a temporary business setback and that her financial situation has since stabilized. She also demonstrates a perfect payment history over the past 24 months, reinforcing her credibility.

With these adjustments, Jessica's profile is transformed. Her lower LTV, improved DTI, strong reserves, and stable income collectively offset her credit challenges. The lender is now able to approve her loan, albeit with a slightly higher interest rate due to her credit score.

This example demonstrates how strategic adjustments can turn an initially unapprovable scenario into a successful outcome. By focusing on compensating factors and understanding how each element of the loan is evaluated, borrowers can take control of the process and achieve their homeownership goals despite past credit challenges.

Chapter 10

Advanced Structuring Strategies for Bank Statement Mortgage Loan Approvals

As you reach this final chapter, you are no longer approaching bank statement mortgage loans as a beginner. You now understand income calculations, LTV strategies, reserves, credit positioning, underwriting, and compensating factors. Chapter 10 brings everything together and elevates your approach to an advanced level—where you are not just qualifying for a loan, but strategically engineering approvals. This is where top-performing borrowers and mortgage professionals separate themselves from the average applicant. They don't leave outcomes to chance—they design them.

Advanced structuring is the process of aligning every element of your loan—income, assets, credit, debt, and property—into a cohesive strategy that maximizes approval probability while optimizing long-term financial outcomes. Instead of reacting to lender requirements, you proactively build a file that fits within multiple approval pathways. This gives you flexibility, leverage, and control throughout the process. One of the most powerful advanced strategies is layering compensating strengths intentionally. Earlier, you learned that lenders evaluate risk holistically. At the advanced level, you begin to "stack" strengths in key areas. For example, combining a lower LTV with strong reserves and a solid credit score can allow for higher DTI tolerance. Similarly, pairing consistent bank statement income with a clean financial structure and documented expense ratios can unlock more favorable income calculations. The goal is not perfection in one category, but strength across several.

Another advanced concept is dual-path qualification. This means structuring your loan so that it could potentially qualify under more than one method or lender guideline. For example, a borrower might qualify using personal bank statements with a standard expense ratio, but also be able to qualify using a CPA-prepared profit and loss statement with a lower expense factor. By preparing both options, you create flexibility. If one path encounters issues during underwriting, you can pivot quickly without restarting the process.

Timing optimization is another critical strategy. Advanced borrowers understand that when you apply can be just as important as how you apply. For instance, timing your application after paying down debt, after a strong deposit cycle, or after increasing your reserves can significantly improve your profile. Similarly, avoiding applications during periods of inconsistent income or large unexplained transactions can prevent unnecessary complications. Strategic timing allows you to present your strongest possible snapshot to the lender.

Income engineering is also a key component of advanced structuring. This does not mean manipulating numbers—it means presenting your income in the most accurate and favorable way within lender guidelines. This can involve choosing between 12-month and 24-month bank statement programs, leveraging business versus personal accounts, or working with a CPA to document expense ratios more effectively. Small adjustments in how income is presented can lead to significant differences in qualifying amounts.

Asset positioning is another area where advanced strategy comes into play. Instead of simply showing enough funds to meet requirements, you structure your assets to maximize their impact. This may involve consolidating accounts, seasoning funds in advance, or allocating assets in a way that strengthens both reserves and down payment simultaneously. Advanced borrowers understand that liquidity is not just about having money—it is about how that money is presented and utilized.

Debt structuring is equally important. Rather than focusing only on reducing debt, advanced borrowers analyze which debts have the greatest impact on DTI and address those strategically. For example, paying off a credit card with a high minimum payment may have a greater impact than paying down a larger loan with a lower payment. In some cases, restructuring debt—such as refinancing or consolidating—can improve monthly obligations and strengthen the overall profile.

Property selection can also influence approval. Not all properties are evaluated equally. Factors such as property type, condition, and location can affect risk assessment. Advanced borrowers consider these elements when selecting a home, ensuring that the property aligns with lender guidelines. Choosing a property that is straightforward and low-risk from an underwriting perspective can simplify the process and reduce potential issues.

Another advanced strategy is pre-underwriting preparation. This involves reviewing your entire financial profile as if you were the underwriter before submitting your application. By identifying potential red flags in advance—such as large deposits, inconsistent income, or credit issues—you can address them proactively. This reduces surprises during underwriting and increases the likelihood of a smooth approval process.

Scenario modeling is a powerful tool at this level. By analyzing different loan structures—varying down payments, interest rates, or income calculations—you can determine the optimal configuration for your situation. This allows you to make informed decisions rather than relying on estimates. Advanced borrowers often evaluate multiple scenarios before committing to a specific strategy.

Flexibility is another hallmark of advanced structuring. Even with careful preparation, unexpected challenges can arise during underwriting. Having backup plans—such as alternative documentation, additional reserves, or adjusted loan terms—allows you to adapt quickly. This flexibility can mean the difference between a delayed approval and a successful closing.

Finally, advanced structuring is about mindset. It requires a shift from thinking like a borrower to thinking like a strategist. You are no longer simply asking, "Can I qualify?" Instead, you are asking, "How can I structure this loan to achieve the best possible outcome?" This mindset empowers you to take control of the process and make decisions that align with your long-term financial goals.

As you complete this book, you now have a comprehensive understanding of bank statement mortgage loans for primary residences. From foundational concepts to advanced strategies, you are equipped to navigate the process with confidence and precision. The knowledge you have gained allows you to move beyond limitations and create opportunities—turning homeownership into a strategic and achievable goal.

Real-Life Math Example: Engineering a Loan Approval Using Advanced Structuring

To demonstrate how advanced structuring strategies work in practice, let's examine a detailed example involving a borrower named Michael, a self-employed entrepreneur seeking to purchase a primary residence.

Michael is purchasing a home for $750,000. He initially plans to put down 15%, or $112,500, resulting in a loan amount of $637,500 and an LTV of 85%. His bank statements show total deposits of $240,000 over 12 months, averaging $20,000 per month. The lender applies a 50% expense factor, resulting in a qualifying income of $10,000 per month.

Michael's estimated monthly housing payment is $4,800. He also has a car payment of $700 and credit card payments totaling $500, bringing his total monthly obligations to

$6,000. Dividing this by his income of $10,000 results in a DTI of 60%, which is above most program limits.

At this stage, Michael's loan is not likely to be approved. However, by applying advanced structuring strategies, he can transform his profile.

First, Michael explores income engineering. He works with a CPA to document a lower expense ratio of 40%, increasing his qualifying income to $12,000 per month. With the same $6,000 in obligations, his DTI drops to 50%, bringing him closer to acceptable limits.

Next, he addresses debt structuring. He pays off his credit card balances, eliminating the $500 monthly payment. His total obligations are now $5,500, reducing his DTI to approximately 46%.

Michael then adjusts his LTV strategy by increasing his down payment to 25%, or $187,500. This reduces his loan amount to $562,500 and lowers his monthly housing payment to approximately $4,200. His total monthly obligations drop to $4,900, resulting in a DTI of approximately 41%.

To further strengthen his profile, Michael demonstrates strong reserves, showing 12 months of housing payments in liquid assets, totaling approximately $50,400. This acts as a powerful compensating factor and increases lender confidence.

Michael also prepares a dual-path qualification strategy. In addition to his bank statement income, he provides a CPA-prepared profit and loss statement that supports his income calculations. This gives the lender flexibility in evaluating his file.

Finally, Michael times his application strategically, ensuring that his most recent bank statements reflect consistent deposits and stable balances. He avoids large transactions or new credit activity during this period, presenting a clean and organized financial profile.

Through these combined strategies, Michael transforms an initially high-risk application into a strong, approvable loan. His DTI is reduced, his LTV is improved, his reserves are strengthened, and his income is optimized. Each adjustment builds on the previous one, creating a cohesive and compelling financial narrative.

This example illustrates the power of advanced structuring. By understanding how each component of the loan interacts with the others, borrowers can take control of the process and engineer successful outcomes. Rather than relying on chance, you can design your loan with precision—maximizing approval, minimizing cost, and aligning your mortgage with your long-term financial goals.

Chapter 11

Closing the Loan and Preparing for Long-Term Financial Success

Reaching the final stages of your bank statement mortgage loan for a primary residence is both exciting and critical. After navigating income structuring, credit optimization, underwriting conditions, and advanced loan strategies, you now arrive at the closing phase—the point where everything becomes official. However, closing is not just the end of the process; it is the beginning of a new financial chapter. The decisions you make at closing and the habits you establish afterward will determine not only the success of your mortgage but also your long-term financial trajectory.

The closing process begins once you receive what is commonly referred to as "clear to close." This means that all underwriting conditions have been satisfied and the lender has approved your loan for final documentation. At this stage, the loan moves into closing preparation, where final numbers are calculated, documents are generated, and a closing date is scheduled. While this may seem straightforward, attention to detail is essential. Even small changes in your financial profile at this point can affect your approval. One of the most important documents you will receive is the Closing

Disclosure, often referred to as the CD. This document outlines the final terms of your loan, including the interest rate, monthly payment, loan amount, closing costs, and cash required at closing. Reviewing this document carefully is crucial. You should compare it to your initial Loan Estimate to ensure that there are no unexpected changes. Understanding every line item empowers you to make informed decisions and avoid surprises.

Cash to close is a key component of this stage. This includes your down payment, closing costs, and any prepaid items such as property taxes and insurance. Ensuring that your funds are properly sourced and transferred is critical. Lenders require that these funds be verified and documented, and last-minute changes can cause delays. It is important to coordinate closely with your lender and closing agent to ensure that all funds are in place before the scheduled closing date.

Another important aspect of closing is final verification. Even after receiving conditional approval, lenders often perform a final review of your credit, employment, and financial status. This may include a soft credit pull to check for new debts or inquiries. It is essential to maintain financial stability during this period. Avoid opening new credit accounts, making large purchases, or transferring significant funds between accounts. Consistency is key to ensuring a smooth closing process. The signing of documents is the formal step where you agree to the terms of the loan. This typically takes place at a title company or with a notary, depending on your location. During this process, you will sign a series of documents, including the promissory note, which outlines your obligation to repay the loan, and the deed of trust or mortgage, which secures the loan against the property. Taking the time to understand these documents reinforces your confidence and ensures that you are fully aware of your commitments.

Once the documents are signed, the loan enters the funding stage. This is when the lender releases the funds to complete the transaction. For purchases, this means transferring funds to the seller. For refinances, it may involve paying off an existing loan and disbursing any remaining funds. After funding, the transaction is recorded with the appropriate local authority, officially transferring ownership or updating the lien on the property.

While closing marks the completion of the loan process, it is equally important to focus on what comes next. Owning a home comes with ongoing financial responsibilities, and managing your mortgage effectively is key to long-term success. Establishing a system for making timely payments is essential. Setting up automatic payments can help ensure consistency and protect your credit profile. Building equity should be a central part of your strategy. Equity represents your ownership stake in the property and grows as you pay down your loan and as the property appreciates in value. Making additional principal payments, even in small amounts, can accelerate equity growth and reduce the total interest paid over the life of the loan. Over time, this can create opportunities for refinancing, accessing equity, or leveraging your property for other investments.

Maintaining strong reserves after closing is equally important. While you may have used a portion of your savings for the down payment and closing costs, rebuilding your reserves provides a financial cushion for unexpected expenses. Homeownership comes with maintenance costs, repairs, and other obligations that require financial flexibility. A strong reserve position ensures that you can handle these challenges without disrupting your financial stability.

Monitoring your credit and financial profile continues to be important after closing. Your mortgage payment history will become a significant factor in your credit profile, and maintaining a perfect payment record can improve your score over time. This positions you for future opportunities, such as refinancing into better terms or qualifying for additional investments.

Refinancing is another strategy to consider as part of your long-term plan. If interest rates decrease, your income improves, or your credit profile strengthens, you may be able to refinance your loan to secure better terms. This can reduce your monthly payment, shorten your loan term, or allow you to access equity for other purposes. Understanding when and how to refinance is a valuable skill that can enhance your financial position.

Tax considerations also play a role in homeownership. Mortgage interest and property taxes may be deductible, depending on your individual situation. Consulting with a tax professional can help you understand how your mortgage fits into your overall tax strategy and identify opportunities for savings.

Finally, mindset is a critical component of long-term success. Owning a home is not just about having a place to live—it is about building a foundation for financial growth. By approaching your mortgage as a strategic tool rather than just a monthly obligation, you can create opportunities for wealth building and financial independence.

This chapter emphasizes that closing is not the end of the journey—it is the beginning. By understanding the closing process and preparing for what comes next, you position yourself for long-term success. The knowledge and strategies you have gained throughout this book empower you to navigate not only the loan process but also the broader financial landscape with confidence and clarity.

Real-Life Math Example: From Closing Costs to Long-Term Wealth Building

To illustrate how closing and post-closing strategies impact financial outcomes, let's examine a detailed example involving a borrower named Daniel, who has just completed a bank statement mortgage loan for his primary residence.

Daniel purchases a home for $600,000 with a 20% down payment of $120,000, resulting in a loan amount of $480,000. His interest rate is 7.0%, and his monthly principal and interest payment is approximately $3,200. Including taxes and insurance, his total monthly housing payment is $3,800.

At closing, Daniel's total closing costs amount to $12,000. Combined with his down payment, his total cash to close is $132,000. After closing, he has $40,000 remaining in savings, which serves as his reserve fund.

Now let's examine Daniel's long-term strategy. First, he decides to make an additional $200 payment toward principal each month. This increases his total monthly payment to $4,000 but has a significant impact on his loan. Over time, this extra payment reduces the loan term and saves him tens of thousands of dollars in interest. Next, we analyze equity growth. In the first year, a portion of Daniel's monthly payment goes toward principal reduction, increasing his equity. If his property appreciates at an average rate of 3% per year, the value of his home increases to approximately $618,000 after one year. Combined with his principal reduction, his total equity grows significantly.

After five years, Daniel's loan balance decreases to approximately $450,000 due to regular payments and additional principal contributions. At the same time, his home's value increases to approximately $695,000 based on continued appreciation. This results in equity of approximately $245,000, a substantial increase from his initial investment.

Now consider refinancing opportunities. If interest rates drop to 5.5% after five years, Daniel can refinance his remaining balance of $450,000 at the lower rate. His new monthly payment decreases significantly, saving him hundreds of dollars per month. Alternatively, he could choose to maintain a similar payment and shorten his loan term, accelerating his path to full ownership.

Daniel also maintains his reserve strategy by rebuilding his savings to $60,000 over time. This provides a financial cushion and allows him to handle unexpected expenses without relying on credit. Additionally, his consistent mortgage payments improve his credit score, positioning him for future financial opportunities.

Finally, Daniel considers leveraging his equity for investment purposes. With $245,000 in equity, he may be able to access a portion of this value through a home equity line of credit or cash-out refinance. This capital can be used to invest in additional properties or other income-generating assets, further expanding his financial portfolio.

This example demonstrates how the decisions made at closing and beyond can shape long-term financial outcomes. By understanding the numbers and applying strategic planning, Daniel transforms his mortgage from a simple obligation into a powerful tool for wealth building. This approach reflects the ultimate goal of this book—to empower you with the knowledge and strategies needed to achieve lasting financial success through homeownership.

Chapter 12

Building a Long-Term Wealth Strategy Using Your Primary Residence

As you reach the final chapter of this book, it is important to shift your perspective from simply obtaining a mortgage to leveraging your primary residence as a long-term financial asset. While many borrowers view their home as a place to live, advanced borrowers understand that it can also serve as a powerful tool for building wealth, creating financial flexibility, and generating future opportunities. When used strategically, your primary residence becomes more than just a liability—it becomes a cornerstone of your financial plan.

The foundation of this strategy begins with understanding equity. Equity is the difference between your property's market value and the remaining balance on your mortgage. As you make payments and as your property appreciates over time, your equity grows. This growth is not just theoretical—it represents real financial value that can be accessed and utilized in various ways. The key is knowing how to build, protect, and leverage that equity effectively.

One of the most straightforward ways to build equity is through consistent mortgage payments. Each payment reduces your loan balance, increasing your ownership stake in the property. While early payments are weighted more heavily toward interest, over time a larger portion goes toward principal. By making additional principal payments, even in small amounts, you can accelerate this process and significantly reduce the total interest paid over the life of the loan.

Appreciation is another major driver of equity growth. Real estate values tend to increase over time, although the rate of appreciation can vary based on location, market conditions, and property characteristics. By purchasing in strong markets and maintaining your property, you can benefit from this natural increase in value. Combining appreciation with principal reduction creates a powerful compounding effect that builds wealth over time.

Once equity has been established, it can be leveraged in several ways. One common method is through a home equity line of credit (HELOC) or a cash-out refinance. These options allow you to access a portion of your home's equity and use it for other purposes, such as investing in additional real estate, starting a business, or consolidating higher-interest debt. The ability to convert equity into liquidity provides flexibility and opens the door to new opportunities. Strategic refinancing is another important tool in long-term wealth building. As your financial profile improves—through higher income, better credit, or lower interest rates—you may be able to refinance your mortgage to secure more favorable terms. This can reduce your monthly payment, shorten your loan term, or free up cash for other investments. Understanding when and how to refinance allows you to adapt to changing market conditions and optimize your financial position.

Another key concept is the idea of "trapped equity." This refers to equity that exists in your home but is not actively being used. While having equity is valuable, it does not generate income on its own. Advanced borrowers look for ways to put this equity to work, either by reinvesting it into income-producing assets or by using it to reduce other financial obligations. The goal is to ensure that your equity contributes to your overall financial growth rather than remaining idle.

Cash flow management also plays a critical role in this strategy. Your mortgage payment is likely one of your largest monthly expenses, and managing it effectively can have a significant impact on your financial health. By optimizing your loan structure, making extra payments when possible, and maintaining strong reserves, you create a stable financial foundation that supports long-term growth.

Diversification is another important principle. While real estate can be a powerful wealth-building tool, it should be part of a broader financial strategy that includes other investments such as stocks, bonds, or business ventures. Using your primary residence as a starting point, you can build a diversified portfolio that balances risk and reward. This approach reduces reliance on a single asset and increases overall financial resilience.

Tax advantages associated with homeownership can also contribute to wealth building. Mortgage interest and property taxes may be deductible, depending on your individual situation. Additionally, gains from the sale of a primary residence may be partially excluded from taxation under certain conditions. Understanding these benefits and incorporating them into your strategy can enhance your overall financial outcome.

Risk management is an essential component of any long-term strategy. This includes maintaining adequate insurance coverage, building reserves, and avoiding over-leveraging your property. While leveraging equity can create opportunities, it also introduces risk. Striking the right balance between growth and stability ensures that your financial strategy remains sustainable.

Another advanced concept is transitioning from a primary residence to an investment property. Over time, as your financial situation evolves, you may choose to convert your primary residence into a rental property and purchase a new home. This allows you to retain the asset while generating income, effectively turning your original home into part of your investment portfolio. This strategy, when executed correctly, can significantly accelerate wealth accumulation.

Mindset is perhaps the most important element of this entire process. Viewing your home as a financial tool rather than just a place to live changes how you approach decisions. Every payment, every improvement, and every financial choice becomes part of a larger strategy. This mindset empowers you to take control of your financial future and make decisions that align with your long-term goals.

As you complete this book, you now have the knowledge and tools to not only secure a bank statement mortgage loan but also to use it as a foundation for building lasting wealth. From understanding income and underwriting to mastering advanced structuring and long-term strategies, you are equipped to navigate the complexities of modern lending and create opportunities that extend far beyond homeownership.

Real-Life Math Example: Turning a Primary Residence into a Wealth-Building Asset

To bring these concepts to life, let's examine a detailed example involving a borrower named Sophia, a self-employed entrepreneur who uses her primary residence as a foundation for long-term wealth building.

Sophia purchases a home for $500,000 with a 20% down payment of $100,000, resulting in a loan amount of $400,000. Her interest rate is 7.0%, and her monthly principal and interest payment is approximately $2,660. Including taxes and insurance, her total monthly housing payment is $3,200.

In the first year, Sophia's payments reduce her loan balance slightly, increasing her equity. At the same time, her property appreciates by 3%, increasing its value to $515,000. Her equity at the end of the first year is approximately $115,000, combining both appreciation and principal reduction.

Sophia decides to accelerate her equity growth by making an additional $200 payment toward principal each month. Over five years, this extra payment significantly reduces her loan balance. At the same time, her property continues to appreciate, reaching a value of approximately $580,000. Her remaining loan balance drops to around $360,000, resulting in equity of approximately $220,000. At this point, Sophia explores leveraging her equity. She obtains a HELOC for $100,000, using a portion of her equity while maintaining a conservative combined loan-to-value ratio. She uses these funds to invest in a rental property that generates positive cash flow. This allows her to expand her portfolio without needing to save for another large down payment.

Over the next five years, Sophia continues to build equity in both properties. Her primary residence appreciates further, and her rental property generates income while also increasing in value. By year ten, her primary residence is worth approximately $670,000, and her remaining loan balance is around $300,000. This results in equity of $370,000 in her primary home alone.

Sophia then considers refinancing her primary residence. With improved credit and lower market interest rates, she refinances her remaining balance at a lower rate, reducing her monthly payment and freeing up additional cash flow. She uses this extra cash to further invest in her portfolio, continuing the cycle of growth.

Throughout this process, Sophia maintains strong reserves, ensuring that she can handle unexpected expenses. She also monitors her financial profile, taking advantage of opportunities to optimize her strategy. By viewing her primary residence as a dynamic asset rather than a static expense, she transforms it into a cornerstone of her wealth-building plan.

This example demonstrates how a primary residence can evolve into a powerful financial tool. By combining equity growth, strategic leveraging, and disciplined financial management, Sophia creates a pathway to long-term wealth and financial independence. This approach reflects the ultimate goal of this book—to empower you to use bank statement mortgage loans not just as a means of homeownership, but as a foundation for building a prosperous future.

Chapter 13

Scaling Your Financial Future—From Primary Residence to Portfolio Growth

By the time you reach this chapter, your perspective on homeownership should be fundamentally different from when you started this book. You are no longer simply a borrower trying to qualify for a mortgage—you are now a strategist who understands how to use financing as a tool to create long-term wealth. Chapter 13 takes this one step further by showing you how to scale beyond your primary residence and begin building a broader financial portfolio using the foundation you have already established.

The journey typically begins with your primary residence, but it does not have to end there. In fact, for many successful investors and entrepreneurs, the primary residence becomes the launching point for a much larger strategy. The equity you build, the credit strength you develop, and the financial discipline you establish all combine to create leverage—both literally and figuratively—that can be used to expand into additional assets.

One of the first concepts to understand when scaling is the idea of "equity recycling." This involves using the equity you have built in your primary residence to fund additional investments. Instead of letting your equity sit idle, you convert it into capital that can be deployed elsewhere. This is often done through a home equity line of credit or a cash-out refinance. By accessing a portion of your equity, you can create opportunities to acquire income-producing assets without needing to save for a new down payment from scratch.

Another important principle is transitioning from consumer mindset to investor mindset. When you purchased your primary residence, your focus may have been on comfort, location, and lifestyle. As you begin to scale, your focus shifts toward cash flow, return on investment, and long-term appreciation. This does not mean abandoning your primary residence—it means using it as a stable base from which to pursue additional opportunities.

Credit plays a critical role in scaling. As you make consistent mortgage payments and manage your financial obligations responsibly, your credit profile strengthens. This improved credit allows you to qualify for additional financing, often with better terms. Maintaining low credit utilization, avoiding unnecessary debt, and preserving a strong payment history are essential for keeping this momentum going. Income growth is another key factor. As a self-employed borrower or entrepreneur, your ability to increase income directly impacts your borrowing capacity. By continuing to grow your business, streamline your operations, and maintain consistent deposits, you enhance your ability to qualify for additional loans. Bank statement lending, in particular, provides flexibility that can be leveraged repeatedly as your income grows.

Debt management becomes increasingly important as you scale. While leveraging debt can accelerate growth, it must be done strategically. Each new loan adds to your overall obligations, and maintaining a manageable debt-to-income ratio is essential. This requires careful planning, including timing new acquisitions and ensuring that each investment contributes positively to your financial position.

Another advanced strategy is portfolio diversification. As you expand beyond your primary residence, you may consider different types of properties or investments. This can include rental properties, short-term rentals, multi-family units, or even commercial real estate. Diversification reduces risk and creates multiple streams of income, enhancing your overall financial stability.

Cash flow is the lifeblood of any scalable strategy. While appreciation and equity growth are important, consistent cash flow provides the financial flexibility needed to sustain and expand your portfolio. When evaluating new opportunities, focusing on properties or investments that generate positive cash flow ensures that your portfolio remains self-sustaining.

Timing and sequencing are also critical. Scaling too quickly without a solid foundation can create financial strain, while moving too slowly can limit growth opportunities. The key is to find a balance—expanding your portfolio at a pace that aligns with your financial capacity and risk tolerance. This often involves setting clear goals and milestones, allowing you to measure progress and adjust your strategy as needed.

Tax planning becomes more significant as your portfolio grows. Different types of investments come with different tax implications, and understanding these can help you optimize your returns. Working with a tax professional can provide insights into deductions, depreciation, and other strategies that enhance your overall financial outcome.

Another important concept is leverage optimization. While leverage can amplify returns, it also increases risk. Advanced borrowers understand how to balance leverage with stability, ensuring that their portfolio can withstand market fluctuations. This includes maintaining reserves, diversifying investments, and avoiding overexposure to any single asset or market.

Exit strategies are an often-overlooked aspect of scaling. While the focus is typically on acquisition, it is equally important to consider how and when you will exit or reposition assets. This can include selling properties, refinancing, or transitioning assets into different uses. Having a clear exit strategy ensures that you can adapt to changing circumstances and maximize your returns.

Mindset once again plays a central role. Scaling your financial future requires discipline, patience, and a willingness to think long-term. It involves making decisions that may not provide immediate gratification but contribute to lasting success. By maintaining a strategic perspective, you can navigate challenges and capitalize on opportunities as they arise.

As you complete this chapter, you should see your primary residence not as an endpoint, but as a starting point. It is the foundation upon which you can build a diversified, income-generating portfolio that supports your financial goals. With the knowledge and strategies you have gained throughout this book, you are equipped to move forward with confidence and create a scalable path to financial independence.

Real-Life Math Example: Scaling from a Primary Residence to a Multi-Property Portfolio

To illustrate how scaling works in practice, let's examine a detailed example involving a borrower named Alex, a self-employed entrepreneur who begins with a primary residence and expands into a multi-property portfolio.

Alex purchases a primary residence for $550,000 with a 20% down payment of $110,000, resulting in a loan amount of $440,000. His monthly housing payment is $3,500. Over five years, Alex's property appreciates at an average rate of 4% per year, increasing its value to approximately $670,000. During this time, his loan balance decreases to $400,000 through regular payments.

At this point, Alex has approximately $270,000 in equity. He decides to access a portion of this equity through a HELOC, obtaining $100,000 in available funds. He uses $80,000 of this amount as a down payment on a rental property priced at $400,000.

The rental property generates $2,800 per month in rental income, while the total monthly expenses, including mortgage, taxes, and maintenance, amount to $2,200. This results in a positive cash flow of $600 per month. This additional income helps offset Alex's overall debt obligations and strengthens his financial position.

Over the next five years, the rental property appreciates to approximately $485,000, and the loan balance decreases to $350,000. This creates additional equity of $135,000 in the rental property. Combined with the continued appreciation of his primary residence, Alex's total equity across both properties exceeds $400,000.

Alex then decides to scale further. Using the equity from his rental property, he secures financing for a second investment property. This property generates $800 per month in positive cash flow, further increasing his income. At this stage, Alex has transitioned from a single homeowner to a multi-property investor with diversified income streams.

Now let's examine the overall financial impact. Alex's portfolio generates a combined cash flow of $1,400 per month from his investment properties. His total equity continues to grow through appreciation and principal reduction. Over time, this creates a compounding effect, where both income and equity increase simultaneously.

Additionally, Alex's improved credit profile and increased income allow him to qualify for better financing terms on future acquisitions. This creates a cycle of growth, where each successful investment enhances his ability to pursue the next opportunity.

Through this example, we see how a primary residence can serve as the foundation for a scalable financial strategy. By leveraging equity, managing cash flow, and making strategic decisions, Alex transforms his initial home purchase into a growing portfolio that supports long-term wealth creation.

This approach demonstrates that homeownership is not just about stability—it is about opportunity. With the right strategies and mindset, your primary residence can become the starting point for a financial journey that extends far beyond a single property, creating a pathway to lasting success.

Chapter 14

Risk Management, Market Cycles, and Protecting Your Financial Future

As you continue to grow from a homeowner into a strategic investor, one of the most important disciplines you must develop is risk management. While previous chapters have focused on qualification, structuring, scaling, and wealth-building, this chapter focuses on protection—protecting your assets, your cash flow, your equity, and your long-term financial stability. Success in real estate and mortgage strategy is not only about how much you can gain, but also about how well you can withstand downturns, uncertainty, and unexpected challenges.

Real estate, like any financial asset, operates within cycles. Markets move through periods of expansion, peak, contraction, and recovery. During expansion, property values rise, lending becomes more accessible, and opportunities appear abundant. At the peak, prices may become inflated, and risk begins to increase. During contraction, values may decline, credit may tighten, and borrowers may face financial pressure. Recovery follows, resetting the cycle and creating new opportunities. Understanding these cycles allows you to make informed decisions and avoid overexposure during high-risk periods. One of the most effective ways to manage risk is through conservative leverage. While leverage allows you to control larger assets with less capital, it also amplifies both gains and losses. Maintaining reasonable loan-to-value ratios ensures that you have sufficient equity to absorb market fluctuations. For example, a borrower with a 70% LTV has a larger buffer than one at 90% LTV. This buffer can be critical during periods of declining property values, as it reduces the risk of being "underwater," where the loan balance exceeds the property value.

Reserves are another cornerstone of risk management. As discussed in earlier chapters, reserves provide a financial cushion that allows you to continue making payments during periods of reduced income or unexpected expenses. In the context of scaling and portfolio growth, maintaining reserves becomes even more important. Each additional property or loan increases your financial obligations, and having sufficient liquidity ensures that you can navigate challenges without being forced to sell assets or take on unfavorable debt.

Cash flow stability is equally important. Properties or financial structures that rely on minimal margins are more vulnerable to disruption. For example, if a rental property barely breaks even, a vacancy or unexpected repair can quickly create financial strain. By prioritizing investments with positive and stable cash flow, you create a buffer that supports your overall financial position. This principle applies not only to investment properties but also to your primary residence, where managing your mortgage payment relative to your income is essential.

Diversification is a key strategy for reducing risk. Relying on a single asset, market, or income source increases vulnerability. By spreading your investments across different property types, locations, or even asset classes, you reduce the impact of any single downturn. For example, owning properties in different markets can protect you from localized economic changes, while maintaining other investments outside of real estate adds an additional layer of security.

Interest rate risk is another factor to consider. Changes in interest rates can affect both your existing loans and your ability to refinance or acquire new properties. Fixed-rate loans provide stability, while adjustable-rate loans introduce variability. Understanding how your loan structure responds to interest rate changes allows you to plan accordingly. In some cases, locking in long-term fixed rates may provide peace of mind, while in others, short-term strategies may be more appropriate.

Insurance is an often-overlooked but essential component of risk management. Adequate property insurance protects against physical damage, while liability insurance protects against legal risks. For those with multiple properties, umbrella policies can provide additional coverage. Ensuring that you are properly insured safeguards your assets and reduces the financial impact of unforeseen events.

Market timing is another aspect of risk management, although it should be approached with caution. Attempting to perfectly time the market is difficult, but being aware of market conditions can help you make more informed decisions. For example, being more conservative during peak pricing periods and more aggressive during downturns can improve long-term outcomes. The goal is not to predict exact market movements but to align your strategy with broader trends.

Exit strategies are a critical part of protecting your financial future. Every investment or property should have a clear plan for how it can be sold, refinanced, or repurposed if needed. This flexibility allows you to respond to changing circumstances and capitalize on opportunities. Without a defined exit strategy, you may find yourself limited in your options during challenging periods.

Stress testing your financial profile is another advanced risk management technique. This involves evaluating how your finances would perform under adverse conditions, such as a loss of income, increased interest rates, or property value declines. By identifying potential vulnerabilities in advance, you can take steps to strengthen your position and prepare for various scenarios.

Behavioral discipline is perhaps the most important factor in risk management. Emotional decision-making—such as overextending during market highs or panicking during downturns—can undermine even the best strategies. Maintaining a disciplined, long-term perspective allows you to navigate market cycles with confidence and consistency.

As you integrate these principles into your financial strategy, you begin to see that risk management is not about avoiding risk entirely—it is about managing it intelligently. By balancing growth with protection, you create a resilient financial structure that can withstand challenges and continue to generate opportunities.

This chapter reinforces the idea that sustainable success is built on a foundation of stability and foresight. By understanding market cycles, managing leverage, maintaining reserves, and planning for uncertainty, you position yourself to not only achieve your goals but to protect them over time.

Real-Life Math Example: Stress Testing and Risk-Proofing a Mortgage Strategy

To demonstrate how risk management works in practice, let's examine a detailed example involving a borrower named Ryan, who owns a primary residence and one investment property.

Ryan's primary residence is valued at $600,000, with a remaining loan balance of $420,000, resulting in an LTV of 70%. His monthly housing payment is $3,600. His investment property is valued at $400,000, with a loan balance of $300,000 and a monthly payment of $2,200. The property generates $2,800 in rental income, producing a positive cash flow of $600 per month.

Ryan's total monthly obligations are $5,800, while his total monthly income, including rental income, is $10,000. This results in a DTI of 58%, which is manageable but requires careful monitoring.

Now let's stress test Ryan's scenario. First, we consider a vacancy in the rental property. If the property is vacant for three months, Ryan loses $8,400 in rental income. During this time, he must cover the $2,200 monthly payment out of pocket, increasing his financial burden. If Ryan has reserves of $30,000, he can comfortably absorb this loss without disrupting his financial stability. Next, we consider a market downturn where property values decline by 10%. Ryan's primary residence drops in value to $540,000, and his investment property decreases to $360,000. His loan balances remain the same, increasing his LTV ratios. For the primary residence, the LTV rises to approximately 78%, and for the investment property, it increases to approximately 83%. While still manageable, this reduces his equity buffer and limits refinancing options.

Now let's analyze interest rate risk. If Ryan has an adjustable-rate mortgage on his investment property and rates increase by 1%, his monthly payment could rise from $2,200 to approximately $2,400. This reduces his cash flow from $600 to $400 per month. While still positive, the margin is smaller, highlighting the importance of maintaining a buffer.

Finally, we evaluate Ryan's reserve strategy. If he increases his reserves from $30,000 to $50,000, he strengthens his ability to handle multiple adverse scenarios simultaneously. This additional liquidity provides flexibility and reduces financial stress.

Through this example, we see how stress testing helps identify potential risks and evaluate the strength of a financial strategy. By analyzing different scenarios—vacancy, market decline, and interest rate increases—Ryan gains a clear understanding of his financial resilience.

This approach allows borrowers to make proactive adjustments, such as increasing reserves, reducing leverage, or improving cash flow. Rather than reacting to challenges as they arise, they are prepared to handle them effectively.

This example reinforces the importance of risk management as a core component of long-term success. By understanding and preparing for potential challenges, you can protect your financial future while continuing to pursue growth and opportunity.

Chapter 15

Mastering the System—From Borrower to Financial Architect

As you arrive at the final chapter of this series, your transformation should be clear. You began as a borrower seeking to understand how to qualify for a mortgage using bank statements. Now, you stand equipped with the knowledge, strategies, and mindset of a financial architect—someone who not only navigates the system but designs outcomes within it. This chapter is about mastery. It is about integrating everything you have learned into a repeatable, scalable system that allows you to control your financial future with intention and precision.

Mastery begins with clarity. You now understand that mortgage lending is not random—it is a structured system governed by guidelines, risk assessments, and financial patterns. Once you understand how lenders think, you can align your financial behavior with their expectations. This alignment is the foundation of consistent approvals. Rather than reacting to lender requirements, you anticipate them. Rather than adjusting under pressure, you prepare in advance. The first step in mastering the system is creating a personal financial framework. This framework includes how you manage income, structure bank accounts, control expenses, and maintain reserves. It is the blueprint that ensures your financial profile remains strong and consistent over time. For example, maintaining clean and consistent bank statement deposits, managing credit utilization, and preserving liquidity are not one-time actions—they are ongoing practices that support long-term success.

Another critical element is repeatability. The strategies you have learned are not limited to a single transaction. They can be applied repeatedly as you grow your portfolio and expand your financial opportunities. Whether you are purchasing your first home, refinancing, or acquiring additional properties, the same principles apply. This repeatability allows you to build momentum, where each successful transaction strengthens your ability to pursue the next.

Leverage becomes a central tool at this stage. You understand how to use debt strategically to acquire assets, build equity, and generate income. However, mastery involves using leverage responsibly. It is not about maximizing debt—it is about optimizing it. This means balancing growth with stability, ensuring that each decision contributes to your overall financial health. Another key aspect of mastery is adaptability. Financial markets, lending guidelines, and economic conditions are constantly changing. What works today may need to be adjusted tomorrow. By staying informed and maintaining flexibility, you can adapt your strategy to align with current conditions. This adaptability ensures that you remain effective regardless of external changes.

Systemization is what separates advanced borrowers from true financial architects. Instead of approaching each transaction individually, you create systems that streamline your process. This can include standardized documentation, organized financial records, and established relationships with lenders and professionals. These systems reduce friction, save time, and increase efficiency, allowing you to focus on strategic decisions rather than administrative tasks.

Relationships also play a significant role in mastery. Building strong connections with mortgage professionals, real estate agents, accountants, and financial advisors creates a network of support and expertise. These relationships provide access to opportunities, insights, and resources that can enhance your strategy. Collaboration becomes a powerful tool for achieving your goals.

Another advanced concept is opportunity recognition. As you deepen your understanding of the system, you begin to see opportunities that others may overlook. This can include identifying undervalued properties, recognizing favorable lending conditions, or leveraging unique financial situations. The ability to recognize and act on these opportunities is a hallmark of mastery.

Long-term vision is essential. Every decision you make should align with your broader financial goals. Whether your objective is financial independence, portfolio growth, or legacy building, your strategy should reflect that vision. This requires discipline and patience, as meaningful results often take time to materialize. By maintaining a clear focus, you ensure that your actions contribute to your desired outcome.

Risk awareness remains a critical component. Even at the highest levels of mastery, risk is always present. The difference is that you now understand how to manage it effectively. By maintaining reserves, diversifying your portfolio, and avoiding overextension, you create a resilient financial structure that can withstand challenges.

Education and continuous improvement are also part of mastery. The financial landscape evolves, and staying informed allows you to refine your strategy and maintain a competitive edge. Whether through reading, networking, or practical experience, ongoing learning ensures that your knowledge remains relevant and effective. Finally, mastery is about mindset. It is about seeing yourself not as someone subject to the system, but as someone who operates within it with confidence and control. This mindset empowers you to make decisions with clarity, act with purpose, and pursue opportunities with conviction.

As you close this book, you now possess a comprehensive understanding of bank statement mortgage loans and how they can be used to achieve your goals. From foundational concepts to advanced strategies, you have developed the tools needed to navigate and master the system. The journey does not end here—it continues as you apply these principles and build upon them over time.

Real-Life Math Example: Designing a Repeatable Wealth-Building System

To illustrate how mastery translates into real-world results, let's examine a detailed example involving a borrower named Daniel, who has evolved into a financial architect using the principles from this book.

Daniel begins with a primary residence valued at $500,000, with a loan balance of $400,000 and a monthly payment of $3,200. Over five years, his property appreciates to $580,000, and his loan balance decreases to $360,000. This results in equity of $220,000. Daniel accesses $100,000 of this equity through a HELOC and uses $80,000 as a down payment for an investment property priced at $400,000. The property generates $2,800 in monthly rental income, with expenses totaling $2,200, resulting in a positive cash flow of $600 per month.

Over the next five years, both properties appreciate. Daniel's primary residence increases in value to $650,000, while his investment property rises to $470,000. His loan balances decrease further, resulting in total combined equity of approximately $360,000.

Daniel then repeats the process. He uses equity from his investment property to acquire a second rental property. This property generates an additional $700 per month in cash flow. At this stage, Daniel's portfolio produces a total of $1,300 per month in passive income.

Now let's examine the compounding effect. Over ten years, Daniel's combined property values increase significantly due to appreciation, while his loan balances decrease through regular payments. His total equity grows to over $500,000, and his monthly cash flow continues to increase as rents rise.

Daniel also optimizes his loan structures by refinancing when interest rates decrease, reducing his monthly payments and increasing cash flow. He maintains strong reserves, ensuring that he can handle vacancies or unexpected expenses without disruption.

By year fifteen, Daniel's portfolio includes his primary residence and multiple investment properties, generating consistent income and significant equity. His financial system is now self-sustaining, with each asset contributing to overall growth.

This example demonstrates how mastery creates a repeatable system. By applying the same principles—leveraging equity, managing cash flow, optimizing loan structures, and maintaining discipline—Daniel transforms his initial home purchase into a scalable and sustainable financial strategy.

The key takeaway is that success is not based on a single transaction, but on the ability to replicate and refine a system over time. With the knowledge and strategies you have gained, you now have the foundation to do the same—designing a financial future that is not only achievable but fully within your control.

Final Thoughts

Turning Knowledge Into Action and Building a Legacy

As you reach the end of this series, it is important to recognize that what you have gained is far more than information. You have developed a complete framework for understanding, navigating, and ultimately mastering one of the most powerful financial tools available today—bank statement mortgage lending. This is not just about qualifying for a loan. It is about unlocking access to opportunities that were once limited by traditional systems and using that access to build a future defined by control, flexibility, and long-term growth.

Throughout this journey, you have learned that the mortgage process is not random or inaccessible. It is structured, predictable, and governed by clear principles. When you understand those principles, you gain the ability to position yourself strategically. You are no longer at the mercy of the system—you are operating within it with intention. You understand how income is evaluated, how credit influences outcomes, how reserves provide security, and how every decision you make contributes to your overall financial profile. This clarity is what transforms uncertainty into confidence.

One of the most important shifts that should occur as a result of this knowledge is the way you view yourself in the process.

You are no longer simply a borrower. You are a decision-maker. You are someone who can design your financial path rather than react to it. This shift in identity is powerful because it changes how you approach every opportunity. Instead of asking whether something is possible, you begin asking how to structure it so that it becomes possible.

The concept of structure has been a recurring theme throughout this book for a reason. Structure is what separates successful outcomes from missed opportunities. Two borrowers with the same income can have completely different results based on how that income is presented. Two individuals with similar credit profiles can receive different loan terms based on how their overall file is positioned. This is not coincidence—it is strategy. And now, it is a strategy you understand and can apply.

Another key takeaway is that preparation is your greatest advantage. The most successful borrowers are not those who scramble to meet requirements at the last minute. They are the ones who prepare in advance, who understand what lenders are looking for, and who align their financial behavior accordingly. Preparation reduces stress, increases efficiency, and creates a smoother path from application to closing. More importantly, it gives you control over the process. You have also learned that flexibility is essential. The financial landscape is constantly evolving, and the ability to adapt is what ensures long-term success. Whether it is adjusting your loan structure, timing your application, or exploring alternative strategies, flexibility allows you to navigate challenges and capitalize on opportunities. This adaptability is not about reacting—it is about staying aligned with your goals regardless of changing circumstances.

As you move forward, it is important to remember that this knowledge is only valuable if it is applied. Understanding concepts without taking action limits your potential. The real transformation occurs when you begin to implement what you have learned. This may start with organizing your bank statements, improving your credit profile, or building your reserves. Each step you take moves you closer to your goals and reinforces the habits that lead to long-term success.

Consistency is another critical factor. Financial success is not achieved through a single decision or transaction. It is the result of consistent actions taken over time. Making your payments on time, maintaining strong financial habits, and continuously improving your profile create momentum. This momentum builds confidence and opens the door to additional opportunities.

It is also important to recognize that challenges are part of the process. Not every transaction will be straightforward, and not every outcome will be immediate. There may be moments where adjustments are needed, where conditions must be met, or where strategies must be refined. These challenges are not setbacks—they are part of the journey. Each obstacle you overcome strengthens your understanding and prepares you for future opportunities.

The concept of long-term thinking cannot be overstated. In a world that often prioritizes immediate results, true financial growth requires patience and discipline. The decisions you make today—how you structure your loan, how you manage your finances, how you build your equity—will have a lasting impact on your future. By focusing on long-term outcomes rather than short-term gains, you create a foundation that supports sustainable success.

Your primary residence, which may have initially been viewed simply as a place to live, should now be seen as a strategic asset. It is a starting point, a foundation, and a tool that can be leveraged to create additional opportunities. Whether you choose to build equity, refinance, or expand into other investments, your home becomes part of a larger financial system that you control.

Equally important is the idea of responsibility. With greater knowledge comes greater responsibility. The ability to access financing, leverage assets, and build wealth must be balanced with careful decision-making. Avoiding unnecessary risk, maintaining reserves, and staying within your financial capacity ensure that your growth is sustainable. Responsible use of these strategies protects not only your assets but also your future.

As you continue to apply these principles, you may find yourself in a position to help others. Whether it is guiding family members, advising clients, or sharing your knowledge within your community, the impact of what you have learned extends beyond your own experience. Teaching others reinforces your own understanding and contributes to a broader culture of financial empowerment.

Legacy is the final and perhaps most meaningful aspect of this journey. The decisions you make today have the potential to influence not only your life but also the lives of those around you. Building equity, creating financial stability, and developing a repeatable system can provide opportunities for future generations. This is where the true value of financial knowledge is realized—not just in personal success, but in the ability to create lasting impact.

As you close this book, take a moment to reflect on how far you have come. From understanding the basics of bank statement loans to mastering advanced structuring strategies, you have gained a comprehensive perspective that few possess. This knowledge is a tool—one that can be used to create opportunities, overcome challenges, and build a future aligned with your goals.

The next step is yours. Apply what you have learned. Take action with confidence. Continue to refine your strategy and expand your understanding. The path ahead is not defined by limitations—it is defined by the choices you make and the strategies you implement.

Your journey does not end here. In many ways, it is just beginning.

How to Get a Personalized Bank Statement Mortgage Review

If you found this book helpful, you may want to see how these strategies apply to your specific financial situation.

Bank statement mortgage lending is highly customized—your deposits, income patterns, expense ratios, credit profile, property type, and long-term goals all play a role in determining what you qualify for and how your loan should be structured.

Every borrower's situation is different. The way your income flows through your accounts, how your business operates, your credit history, the property you are purchasing or refinancing, and current lender guidelines all impact your options. The strategies and examples in this book are designed to teach you how bank statement mortgage loans work—but your actual qualifying income, loan amount, and loan structure can only be determined by analyzing your real financial profile.

If you would like a no-obligation Bank Statement Mortgage review, you can request one here:

Email: info@FinibiMortgage.com

A licensed mortgage broker will review your bank statements, income structure, credit profile, and goals, and explain what bank statement mortgage options may be available to you—including:

• 12-month and 24-month bank statement programs• Personal vs business bank statement qualification• Primary residence and investment property financing• Cash-out refinance and equity access strategies• Advanced structuring to maximize qualifying income

No cost. No pressure. No obligation.

Sincerely,

Joseph G. Correa

Finibi Mortgage Inc.

Licensed Mortgage Broker

About the Author

Joseph G. Correa is a licensed mortgage broker and the founder of Finibi Mortgage, a Florida-based brokerage specializing in bank statement mortgage loans, non-QM lending, and strategic real estate financing solutions for self-employed borrowers, entrepreneurs, and investors.

With more than two decades of experience in mortgage lending, underwriting, and deal structuring, Joseph has helped thousands of clients qualify for real estate using alternative income documentation, unlocking opportunities that traditional lending often restricts.

Unlike traditional loan officers who rely strictly on tax returns and W-2 income, Joseph's approach focuses on real cash flow, income structuring, and financial strategy. He believes that borrowers should not be limited by how income is reported on paper, but instead empowered by how income is actually earned and managed.

Joseph is widely recognized for his expertise in:

• Bank statement mortgage loans• Self-employed borrower financing• Non-QM and alternative income lending• Investment property and portfolio financing• Cash-out refinance and equity strategies• Advanced mortgage loan structuring

Through his education platform, Finibi Academy, Joseph has trained tens of thousands of students worldwide in mortgage strategy, real estate investing, credit optimization, and financial independence.

He created the **Bank Statement Mortgage Loan Mastery Series** to provide a clear, step-by-step roadmap for borrowers and professionals who want to qualify for real estate without relying on traditional income documentation.

His mission is simple: To help people use their real income—not just their tax returns—to qualify, invest, and build long-term wealth.

When he is not structuring loans or writing, Joseph works with clients across the United States to design customized mortgage strategies that align with their financial goals, income structure, and long-term investment plans.

The Bank Statement Mortgage Loan Mastery Series Roadmap

The Complete Guide to Qualifying for Real Estate Using Bank Statements Instead of Tax Returns

The purpose of the **Bank Statement Mortgage Loan Mastery Series** is to give borrowers, investors, and mortgage professionals the exact strategies used by lenders and underwriters—translated into simple, practical steps you can apply in real life.

This series takes you from beginner to advanced mastery of how to qualify, structure, and scale real estate financing using bank statements instead of traditional income.

Each book builds on the last. You are not just learning how to get approved—you are learning how to control your approvals.

Book 1 — Bank Statement Mortgage Loan Fundamentals

Learn how bank statement loans work, how income is calculated, and why tax returns are no longer required for many borrowers.

Book 2 — Personal Bank Statement Mortgage Loans

Learn how to qualify using personal accounts, structure

deposits, and maximize usable income.

Book 3 — Business Bank Statement Mortgage Loans

Understand how lenders analyze business revenue, apply expense ratios, and use P&Ls.

Book 4 — Bank Statement Loans for Self-Employed Borrowers

Master how entrepreneurs qualify and structure income for approval.

Book 5 — Bank Statement Loans for Primary Residences

Learn how to buy or refinance your home using bank statement income.

Book 6 — Bank Statement Loans for Investment Properties

Discover how to scale rental portfolios using bank statement + DSCR strategies.

Book 7 — Jumbo Bank Statement Mortgage Loans

Learn how to finance high-value properties with advanced requirements and structuring.

Book 8 — Bank Statement Loan Refinancing & Cash-Out Strategies

Unlock equity, reduce payments, and reinvest capital using bank statement refinancing.

Book 9 — Bank Statement Loans with Credit Challenges

Learn how to qualify even with lower credit using compensating factors and strategy.

Book 10 — Advanced Bank Statement Mortgage Loan Structuring

Engineer approvals using deposits, expense ratios, and lender guidelines.

This series is designed to move you from understanding → execution → mastery.

By the end, you will not just know how to qualify—you will know how to structure deals like a professional.

Educational & Financial Disclaimer

The **Bank Statement Mortgage Loan Mastery Series** is intended for educational and informational purposes only.

This content is designed to help readers understand bank statement mortgage lending, real estate financing strategies, and income structuring concepts. It is not financial, legal, tax, or investment advice.

Joseph G. Correa and Live Stronger Faster are not acting as your personal financial advisor, attorney, accountant, or mortgage professional through this publication.

Mortgage guidelines, underwriting standards, interest rates, and loan programs vary by lender and may change at any time without notice.

All examples in this series are for illustration purposes only and do not guarantee approval or results.

Always consult with licensed professionals before making financial decisions.

Risk Disclosure

Bank statement mortgage lending and real estate investing involve risk.

Income fluctuations, interest rate changes, market conditions, and lender guidelines can all impact loan approval and financial outcomes.

Borrowing against real estate or using leverage increases both potential returns and risks.

Failure to repay a loan may result in foreclosure and loss of property.

Cash flow, rental income, and appreciation are not guaranteed.

All strategies in this series are educational and must be evaluated based on your individual financial situation.

You are solely responsible for your financial decisions.

www.ingramcontent.com/pod-product-compliance
Lightning Source LLC
LaVergne TN
LVHW022224200926
848481LV00006B/2107